AND A
WOODSTOCK
IN A
BIRCH TREE

Titan Facsimile Editions by Charles M. Schulz

Peanuts®
More Peanuts®
Good Grief, more Peanuts®!
Good Ol' Charlie Brown
Snoopy
You're Out of your Mind, Charlie Brown!
But We Love You, Charlie Brown
Peanuts® Revisited
Go Fly a Kite, Charlie Brown
Peanuts® Every Sunday
Snoopy, Come Home
Sunday's Fun Day, Charlie Brown
It's a Dog's Life, Charlie Brown
And a Woodstock in a Birch Tree

AND A WOODSTOCK IN A BIRCH TREE

by Charles M. Schulz

TITAN COMICS

ORIGINALLY BY HOLT, RINEHART AND WINSTON.

PUBLISHED SIMULTANEOUSLY IN CANADA BY HOLT, RINEHART AND WINSTON OF CANADA, LIMITED.

FIRST PUBLISHED IN BOOK FORM IN 1979.

FACSIMILE EDITION PUBLISHED JULY 2022 BY TITAN COMICS,
A DIVISION OF TITAN PUBLISHING GROUP, LTD.
144 SOUTHWARK STREET, LONDON SE1 0UP.

LIBRARY OF CONGRESS CATALOG CARD NUMBER: 79-1926

ISBN: 9781787737075
PRINTED IN INDIA
10 9 8 7 6 5 4 3 2 1

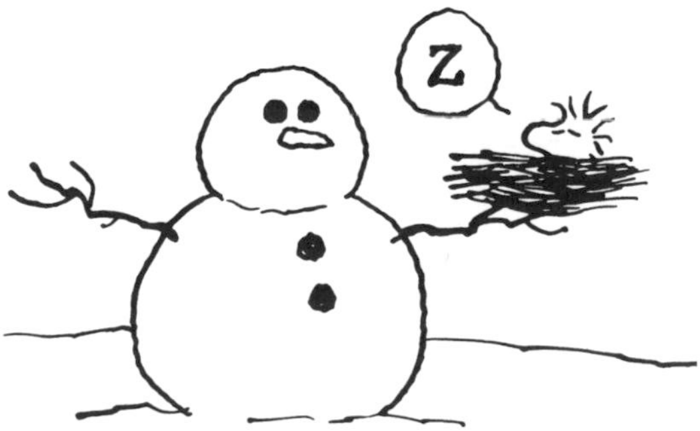
Z

THIS IS HARD ON US LUNGS

IF I START COMPLAINING, YOU'RE ALL IN TROUBLE

SHUT UP, HEART!

WHY DO WE FEET HAVE TO DO ALL THE WORK?

HOW ABOUT TOES? YOU THINK IT'S EASY BEING A TOE?

YOU GUYS ARE ALWAYS COMPLAINING.. WE EARS CAN HEAR YOU WAY UP HERE!

BESIDES, IT'S US LEGS WHO REALLY DO THE RUNNING...

ALL I KNOW IS, RUNNING IS HARD ON THE BACK... BACKS SHOULD BE HOME IN BED...

HOW ABOUT NOSES? I HATE JOKES ABOUT RUNNING NOSES!

LIPS ARE MADE FOR KISSING, NOT RUNNING...WE NEED MORE KISSING...

I'M HUNGRY!

HA! I KNEW THE STOMACH WOULD START COMPLAINING PRETTY SOON! WE ARMS NEVER COMPLAIN

THAT'S A LAUGH! IF IT ISN'T BURSITIS, IT'S TENNIS ELBOW! WE STILL SAY IT'S WE FEET WHO DO ALL THE WORK...

YOU THINK IT'S EASY BEING A FINGER?

HA! JUST TRY BEING AN ELBOW SOMETIME!

HOW CAN THE LONG-DISTANCE RUNNER EVER GET LONELY?

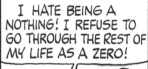

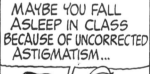

HAVE YOU MADE AN APPOINTMENT WITH AN OPHTHALMOLOGIST YET, SIR?

I DON'T WANT TO BE TOLD THAT I HAVE TO WEAR GLASSES, MARCIE!

YOU COULD BE SQUINTING AND NOT EVEN KNOW IT, SIR.. THAT CAN CAUSE EYE FATIGUE, AND MAKE YOU SLEEPY...

BESIDES, IF YOU WORE GLASSES, YOU MIGHT LOOK LIKE ELTON JOHN!

YES, DOCTOR..A FRIEND OF MINE SUGGESTED I COME TO SEE YOU...

WELL, I'VE BEEN HAVING TROUBLE STAYING AWAKE IN CLASS, AND SHE THINKS IT MIGHT BE BECAUSE OF MY EYES

AN EXAMINATION? YES, SIR...

HOW LONG DO I HAVE TO LIVE, DOC?

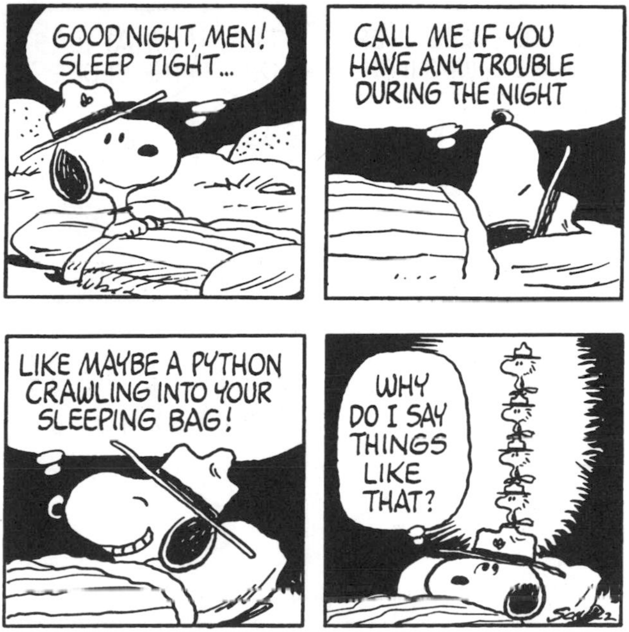
GOOD NIGHT, MEN! SLEEP TIGHT...
CALL ME IF YOU HAVE ANY TROUBLE DURING THE NIGHT
LIKE MAYBE A PYTHON CRAWLING INTO YOUR SLEEPING BAG!
WHY DO I SAY THINGS LIKE THAT?

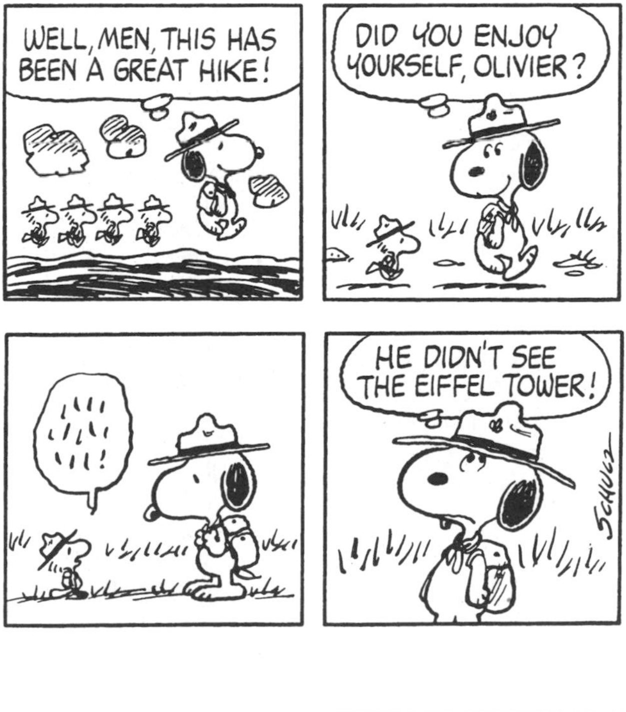
WELL, MEN, THIS HAS BEEN A GREAT HIKE!
DID YOU ENJOY YOURSELF, OLIVIER?
HE DIDN'T SEE THE EIFFEL TOWER!
SCHULZ

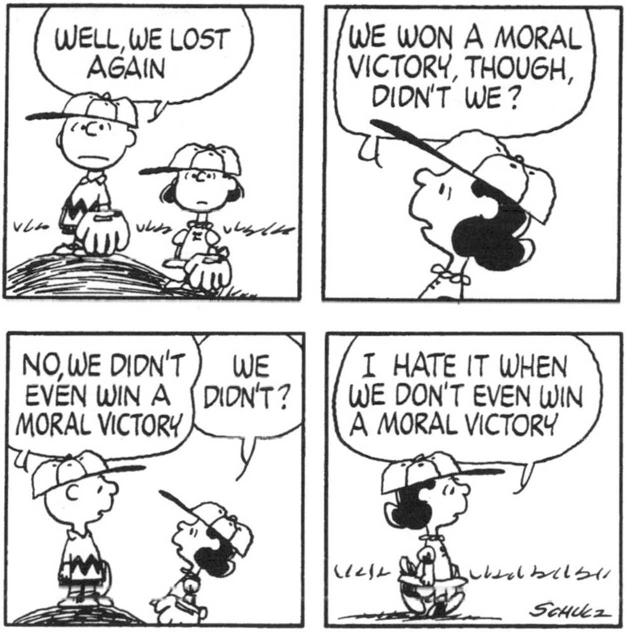
WELL, WE LOST AGAIN
WE WON A MORAL VICTORY, THOUGH, DIDN'T WE?
NO, WE DIDN'T EVEN WIN A MORAL VICTORY
WE DIDN'T?
I HATE IT WHEN WE DON'T EVEN WIN A MORAL VICTORY
SCHULZ

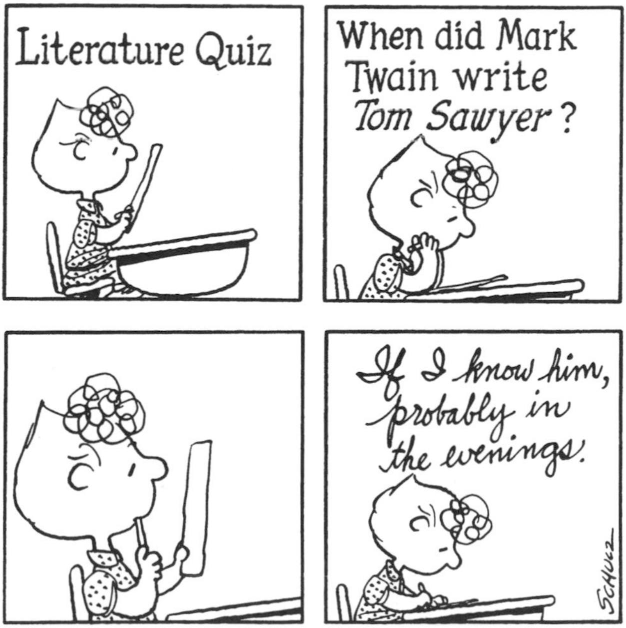
Literature Quiz
When did Mark Twain write *Tom Sawyer*?
If I know him, probably in the evenings.
SCHULZ

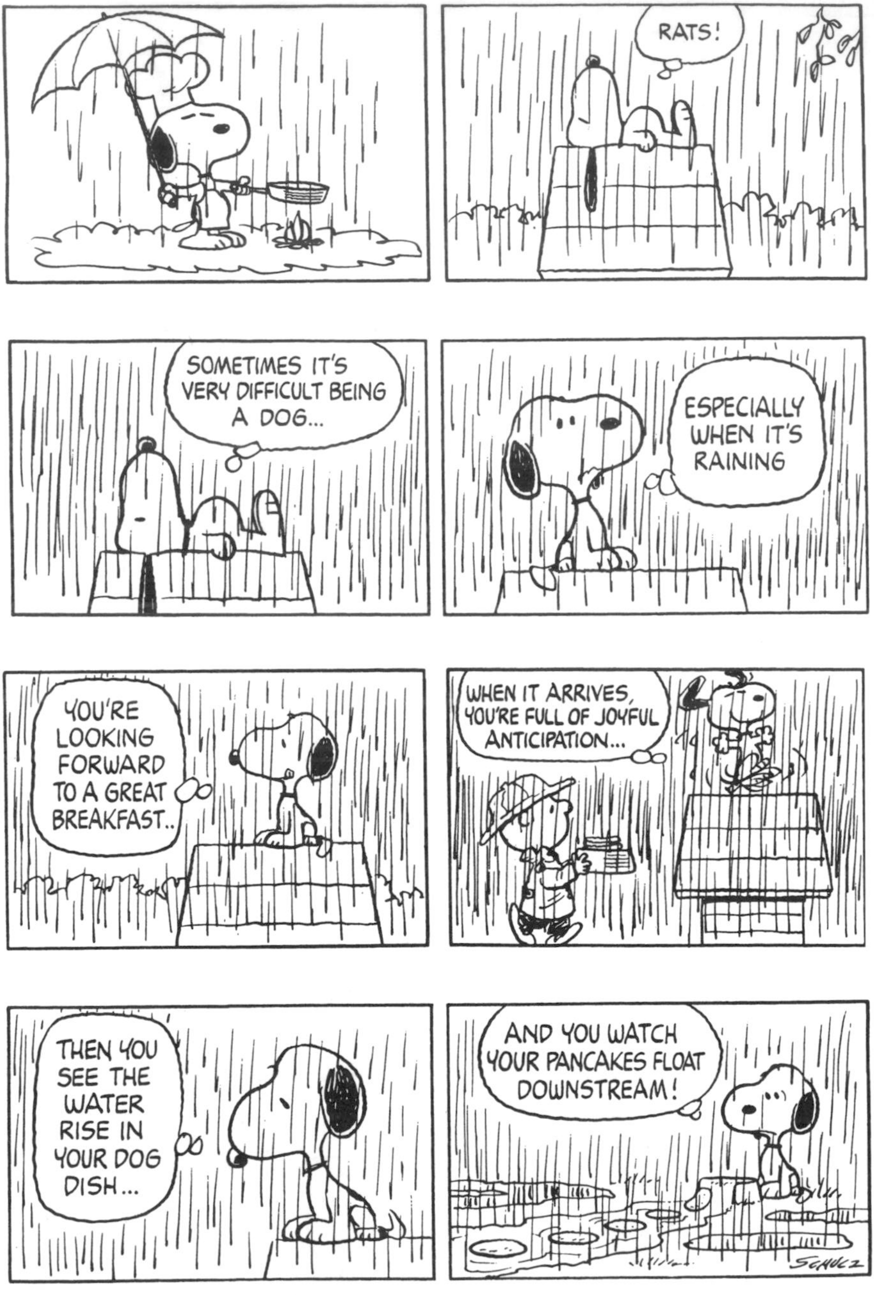
RATS!
SOMETIMES IT'S VERY DIFFICULT BEING A DOG...
ESPECIALLY WHEN IT'S RAINING
YOU'RE LOOKING FORWARD TO A GREAT BREAKFAST..
WHEN IT ARRIVES, YOU'RE FULL OF JOYFUL ANTICIPATION...
THEN YOU SEE THE WATER RISE IN YOUR DOG DISH...
AND YOU WATCH YOUR PANCAKES FLOAT DOWNSTREAM!
SCHULZ

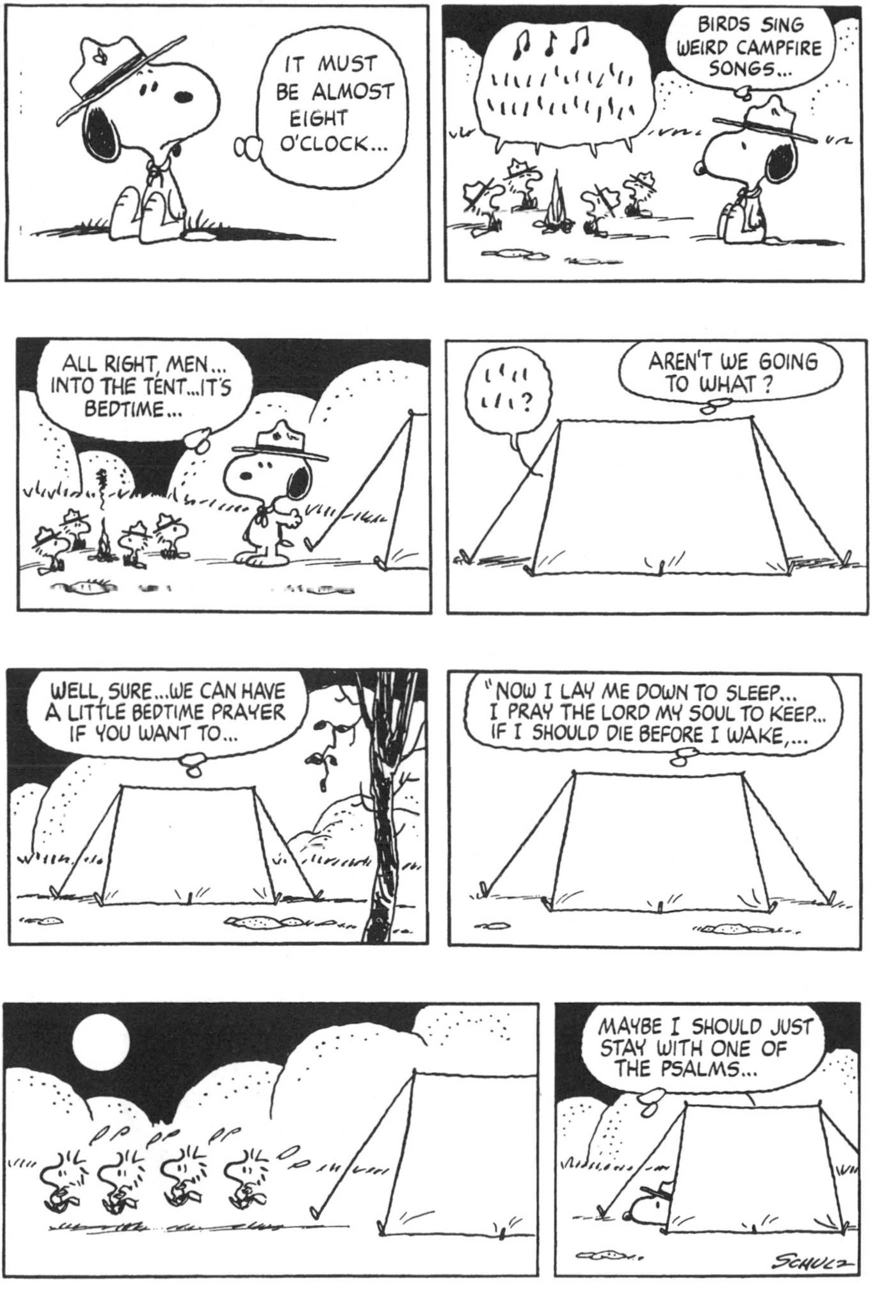
IT MUST BE ALMOST EIGHT O'CLOCK...
BIRDS SING WEIRD CAMPFIRE SONGS...
ALL RIGHT, MEN... INTO THE TENT...IT'S BEDTIME...
?
AREN'T WE GOING TO WHAT ?
WELL, SURE...WE CAN HAVE A LITTLE BEDTIME PRAYER IF YOU WANT TO...
"NOW I LAY ME DOWN TO SLEEP... I PRAY THE LORD MY SOUL TO KEEP... IF I SHOULD DIE BEFORE I WAKE,...
MAYBE I SHOULD JUST STAY WITH ONE OF THE PSALMS...
SCHULZ

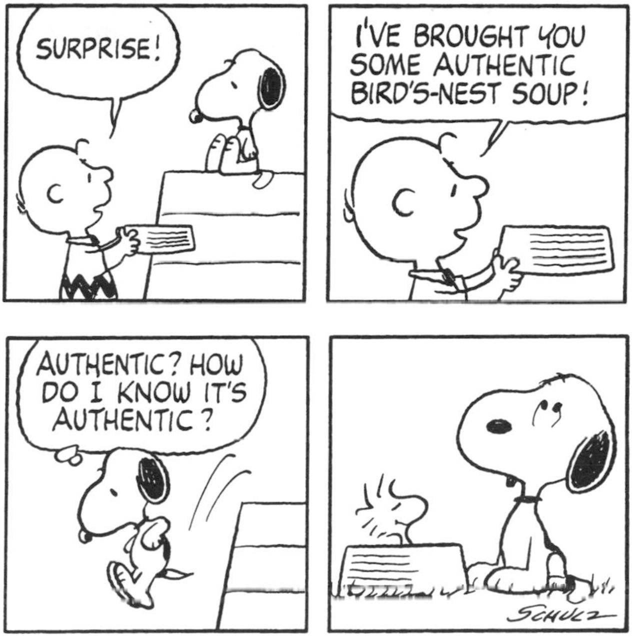
SURPRISE!
I'VE BROUGHT YOU SOME AUTHENTIC BIRD'S-NEST SOUP!
AUTHENTIC? HOW DO I KNOW IT'S AUTHENTIC?
SCHULZ

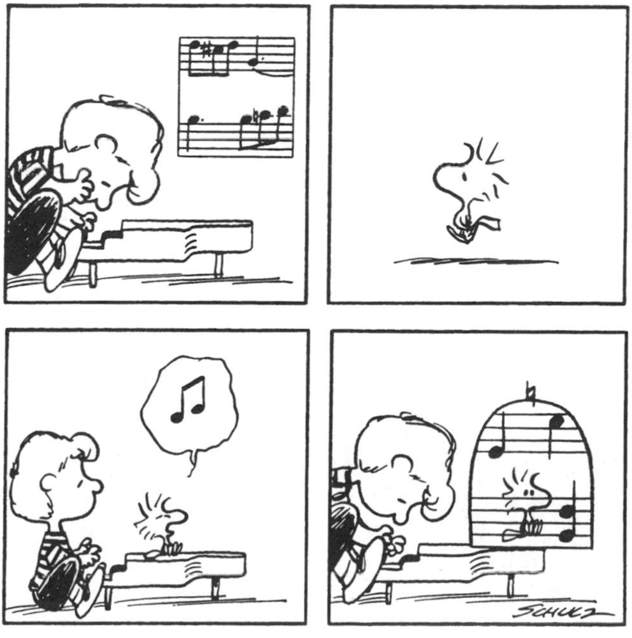
SCHULZ

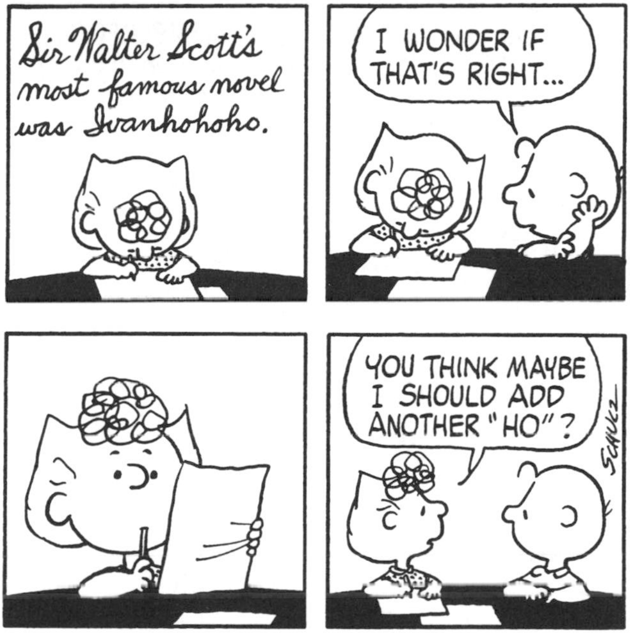
Sir Walter Scott's most famous novel was Ivanhohoho.
I WONDER IF THAT'S RIGHT...
YOU THINK MAYBE I SHOULD ADD ANOTHER "HO"?
SCHULZ

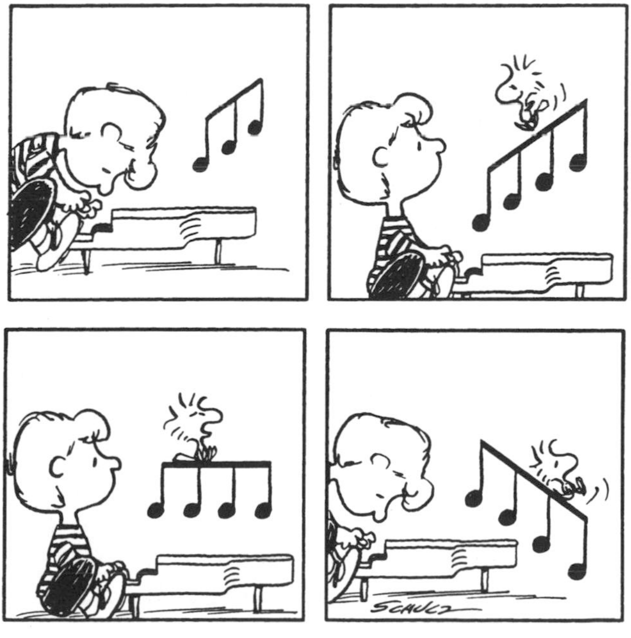
SCHULZ

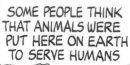

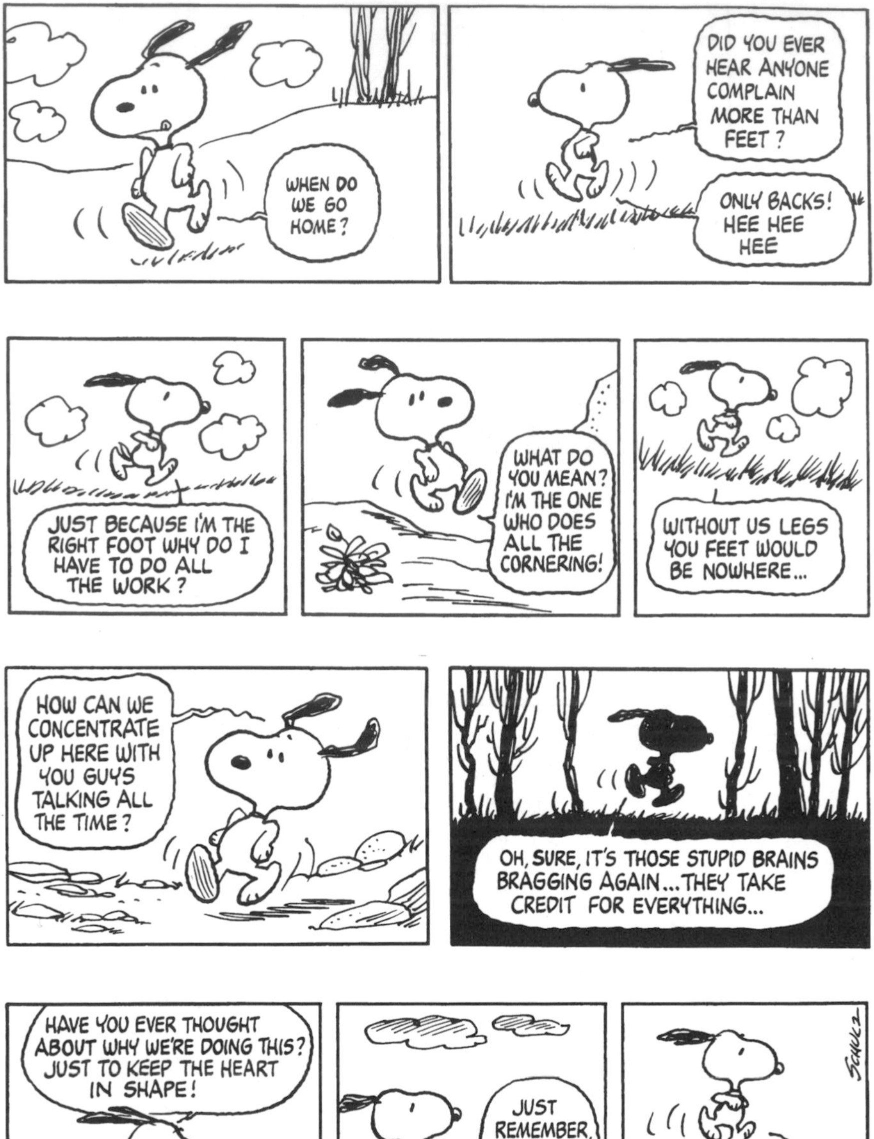
WHEN DO WE GO HOME?
DID YOU EVER HEAR ANYONE COMPLAIN MORE THAN FEET?
ONLY BACKS! HEE HEE HEE
JUST BECAUSE I'M THE RIGHT FOOT WHY DO I HAVE TO DO ALL THE WORK?
WHAT DO YOU MEAN? I'M THE ONE WHO DOES ALL THE CORNERING!
WITHOUT US LEGS YOU FEET WOULD BE NOWHERE...
HOW CAN WE CONCENTRATE UP HERE WITH YOU GUYS TALKING ALL THE TIME?
OH, SURE, IT'S THOSE STUPID BRAINS BRAGGING AGAIN... THEY TAKE CREDIT FOR EVERYTHING...
HAVE YOU EVER THOUGHT ABOUT WHY WE'RE DOING THIS? JUST TO KEEP THE HEART IN SHAPE!
JUST REMEMBER, BOYS, IF I GO, YOU ALL GO!
SCHULZ
THAT'S SCARY!
SHUT UP, AND KEEP RUNNING!

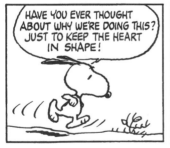

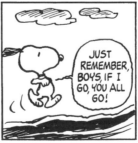

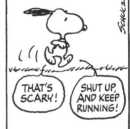

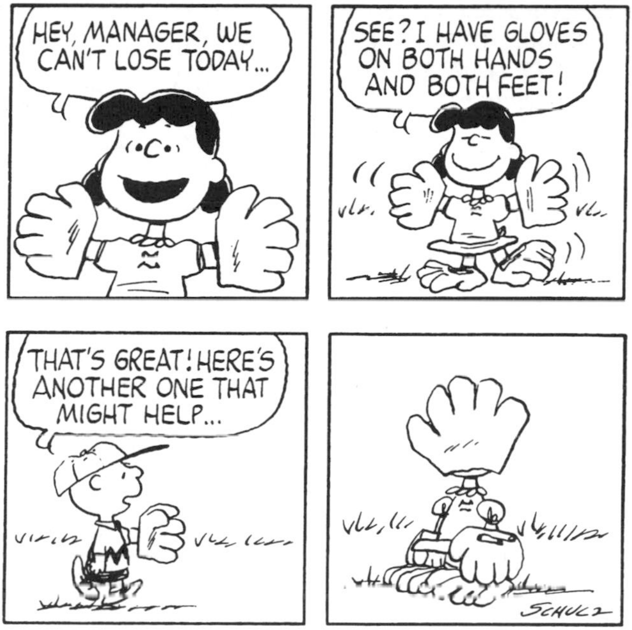
HEY, MANAGER, WE CAN'T LOSE TODAY...
SEE? I HAVE GLOVES ON BOTH HANDS AND BOTH FEET!
THAT'S GREAT! HERE'S ANOTHER ONE THAT MIGHT HELP...
SCHULZ

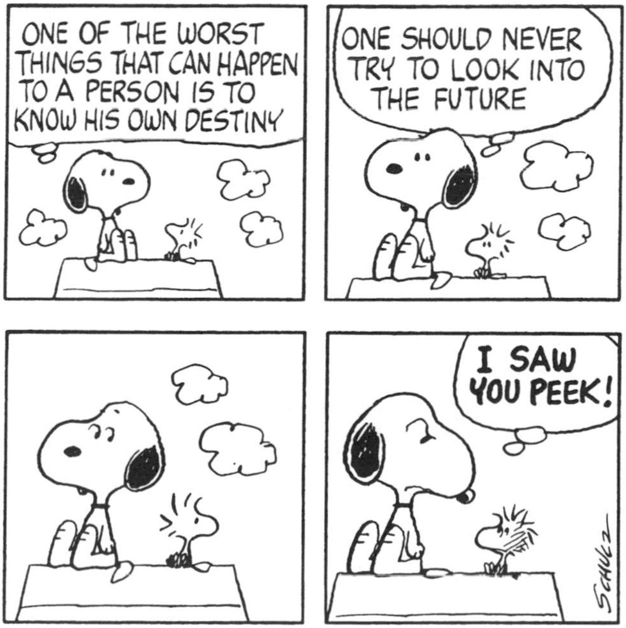
ONE OF THE WORST THINGS THAT CAN HAPPEN TO A PERSON IS TO KNOW HIS OWN DESTINY
ONE SHOULD NEVER TRY TO LOOK INTO THE FUTURE
I SAW YOU PEEK!
SCHULZ

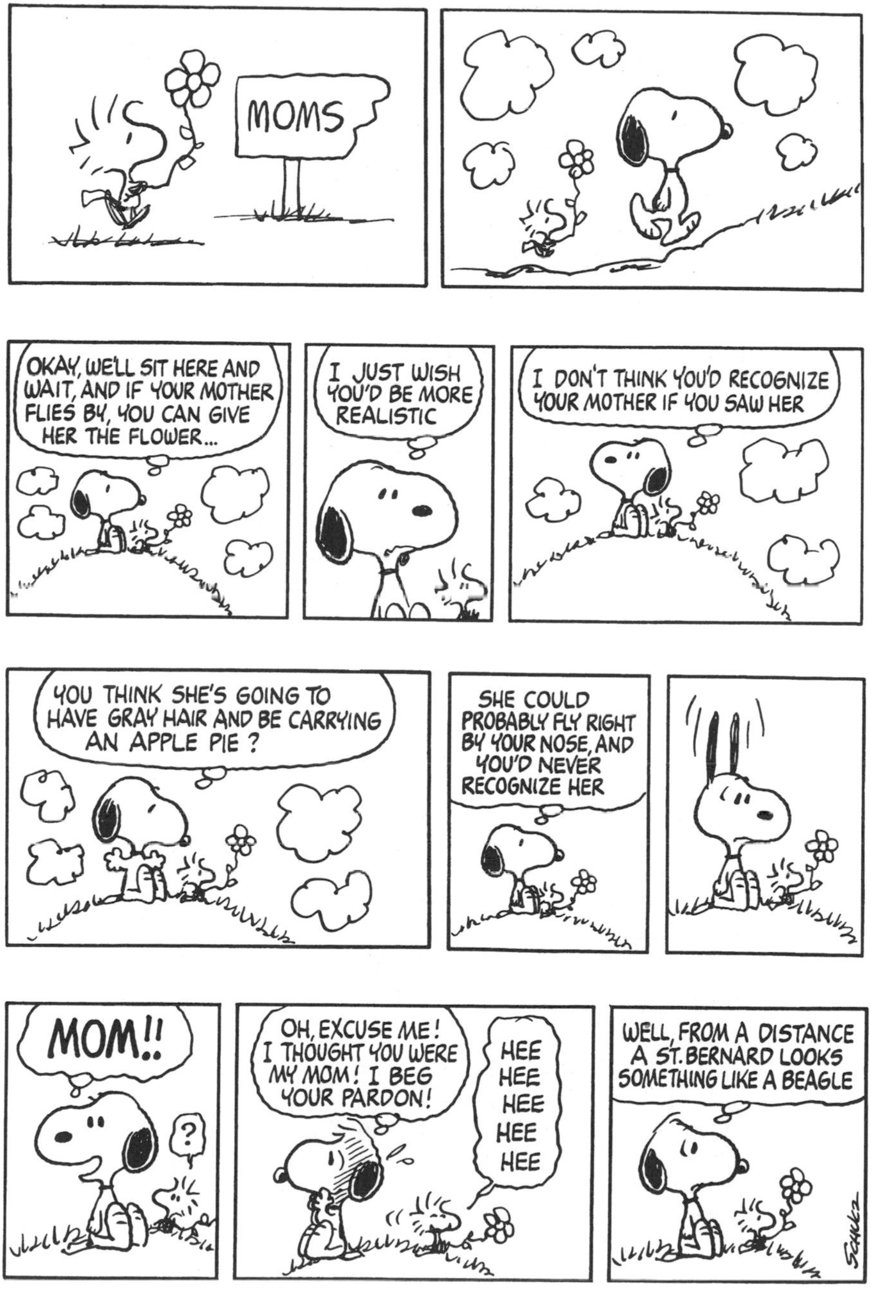
MOMS
OKAY, WE'LL SIT HERE AND WAIT, AND IF YOUR MOTHER FLIES BY, YOU CAN GIVE HER THE FLOWER...
I JUST WISH YOU'D BE MORE REALISTIC
I DON'T THINK YOU'D RECOGNIZE YOUR MOTHER IF YOU SAW HER
YOU THINK SHE'S GOING TO HAVE GRAY HAIR AND BE CARRYING AN APPLE PIE ?
SHE COULD PROBABLY FLY RIGHT BY YOUR NOSE, AND YOU'D NEVER RECOGNIZE HER
MOM!!
?
OH, EXCUSE ME! I THOUGHT YOU WERE MY MOM! I BEG YOUR PARDON!
HEE HEE HEE HEE HEE
WELL, FROM A DISTANCE A ST. BERNARD LOOKS SOMETHING LIKE A BEAGLE
SCHULZ

LUCY, DEAR SISTER!

I ALMOST BOUGHT YOU A BIRTHDAY PRESENT JUST NOW

I SAW THIS BOTTLE OF COLOGNE IN A STORE WINDOW, AND IT ONLY COST A DOLLAR...

I KNEW IT WOULD MAKE YOU HAPPY TO GET IT, BUT THEN I SAW SOMETHING THAT I KNEW WOULD MAKE YOU EVEN MORE HAPPY!

IN THE WINDOW OF THE STORE NEXT DOOR, THERE WAS A SALAMI SANDWICH WHICH ALSO COST A DOLLAR...NOW, I KNOW HOW CONCERNED YOU ARE FOR THE PEOPLES OF THIS WORLD...

I KNOW HOW HAPPY IT'S GOING TO MAKE YOU WHEN I BECOME A FAMOUS DOCTOR, AND CAN HELP THE PEOPLE OF THE WORLD

BUT IF I'M GOING TO BECOME A DOCTOR, I'M GOING TO HAVE TO GET GOOD GRADES IN SCHOOL...

AND TO GET GOOD GRADES, I'M GOING TO HAVE TO STUDY, AND IN ORDER TO STUDY, I HAVE TO BE HEALTHY...

IN ORDER TO BE HEALTHY, I HAVE TO EAT...SO INSTEAD OF THE COLOGNE, I BOUGHT THE SANDWICH...ALL FOR YOUR HAPPINESS!

I'M SO HAPPY I COULD CRY!

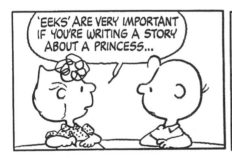
EEK! EEK! EEK!

I'M PRACTICING MY 'EEKS'

'EEKS'?

'EEKS' ARE VERY IMPORTANT IF YOU'RE WRITING A STORY ABOUT A PRINCESS...

SAY THERE'S THIS BEAUTIFUL PRINCESS WHO LIVES IN A CASTLE...SHE'S SITTING AT HER LOOM ONE DAY WHEN SUDDENLY A MOUSE RUNS ACROSS THE FLOOR...

"EEK!"
SHE CRIES...

IF YOU'RE DOING A STORY ABOUT A PRINCESS, YOU HAVE TO BE ABLE TO WRITE A GOOD 'EEK'

AN 'AWK' PROBABLY WOULD HAVE KILLED ME!

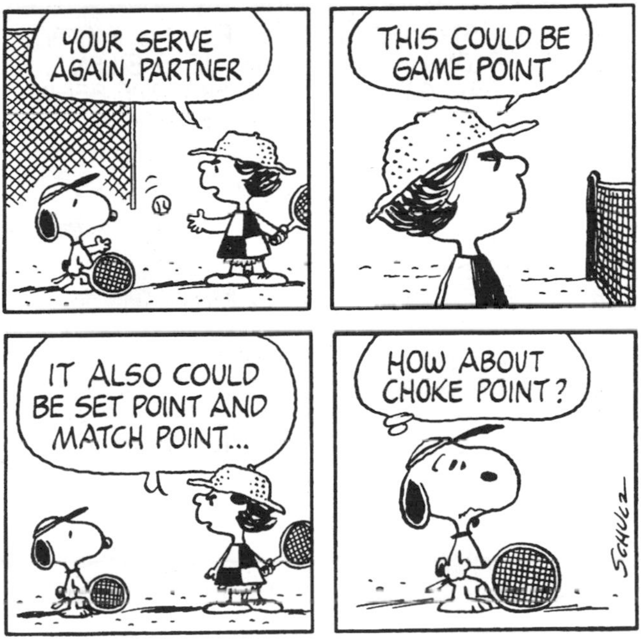
YOUR SERVE AGAIN, PARTNER
THIS COULD BE GAME POINT
IT ALSO COULD BE SET POINT AND MATCH POINT...
HOW ABOUT CHOKE POINT?

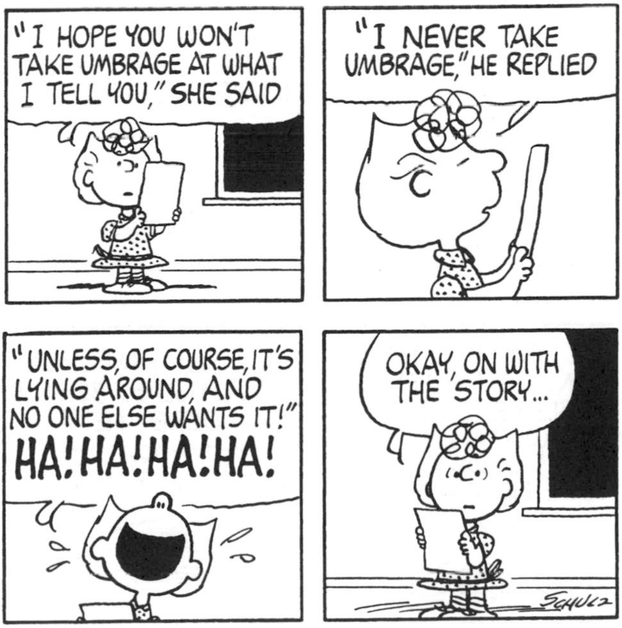
"I HOPE YOU WON'T TAKE UMBRAGE AT WHAT I TELL YOU," SHE SAID
"I NEVER TAKE UMBRAGE," HE REPLIED
"UNLESS, OF COURSE, IT'S LYING AROUND, AND NO ONE ELSE WANTS IT!"
HA! HA! HA! HA!
OKAY, ON WITH THE STORY...

"WRITE A THOUSAND-WORD ESSAY ON LOUIS XIV AND HIS ESTABLISHMENT OF THE ACADÉMIE ROYALE de DANSE"

"IDENTIFY REFERENCES AND SOURCE MATERIAL BY CHAPTER AND PAGE"

NO, MA'AM, I'M NOT SLEEPING...

I JUST PASSED OUT!

I'M ALWAYS THINKING ABOUT THAT LITTLE RED HAIRED GIRL, BUT I KNOW SHE DOESN'T THINK OF ME

SHE DOESN'T THINK OF ME BECAUSE I'M A NOTHING, AND YOU CAN'T THINK OF NOTHING!

YOU'RE NOT REALLY A NOTHING, CHARLIE BROWN

ALMOST

DOES A GIRL EVER GO AROUND THINKING OF A .00001 ?!

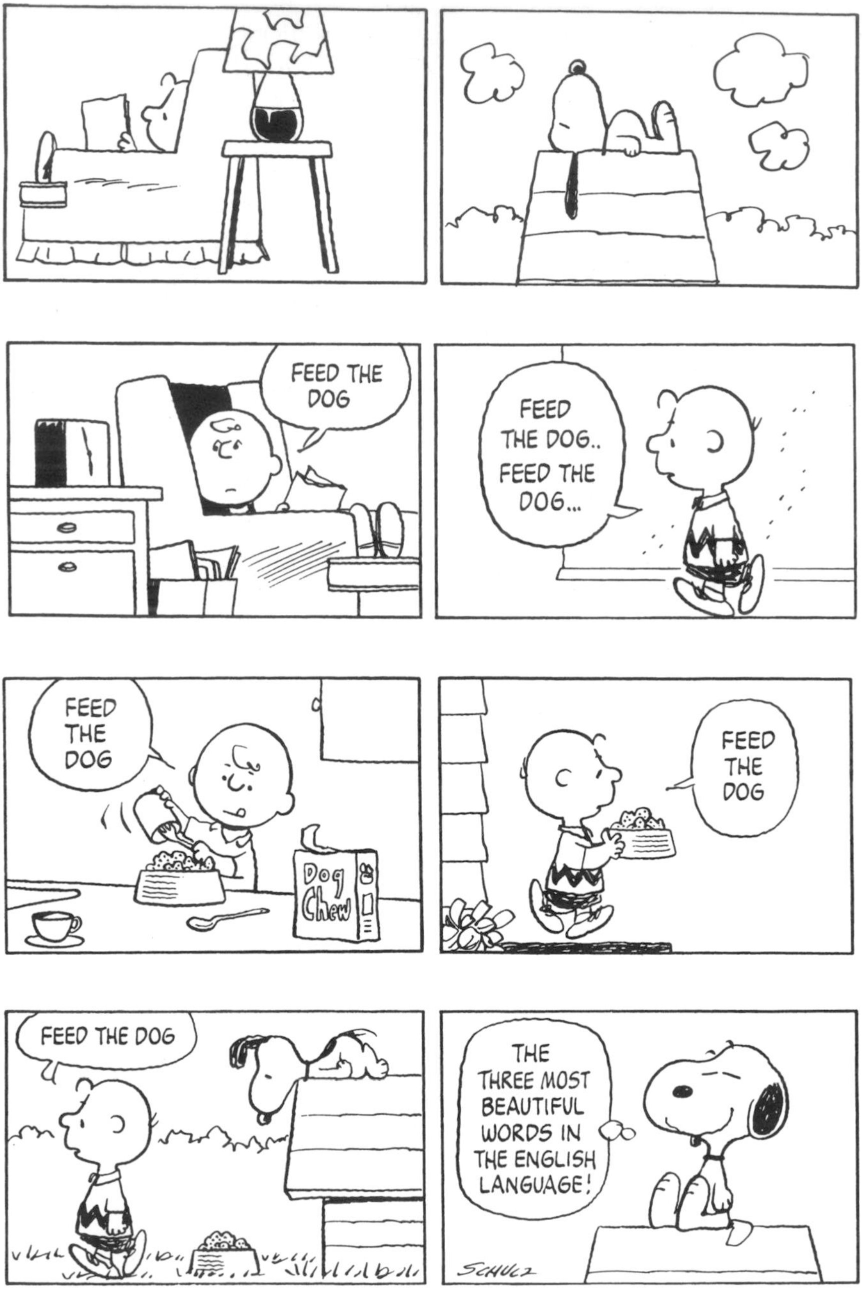
FEED THE DOG
FEED THE DOG.. FEED THE DOG...
FEED THE DOG
Dog Chew
FEED THE DOG
FEED THE DOG
THE THREE MOST BEAUTIFUL WORDS IN THE ENGLISH LANGUAGE!
SCHULZ

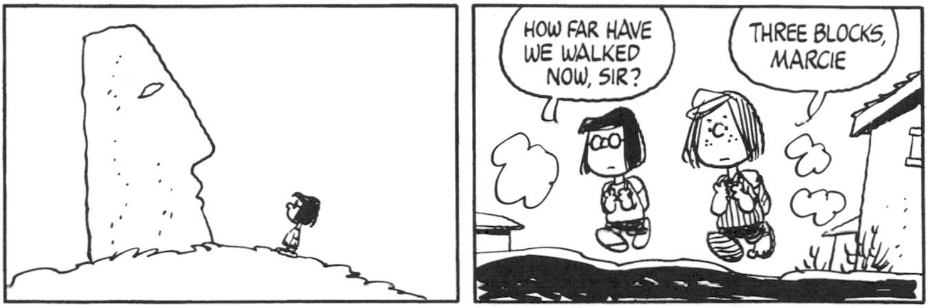
HOW FAR HAVE WE WALKED NOW, SIR?
THREE BLOCKS, MARCIE

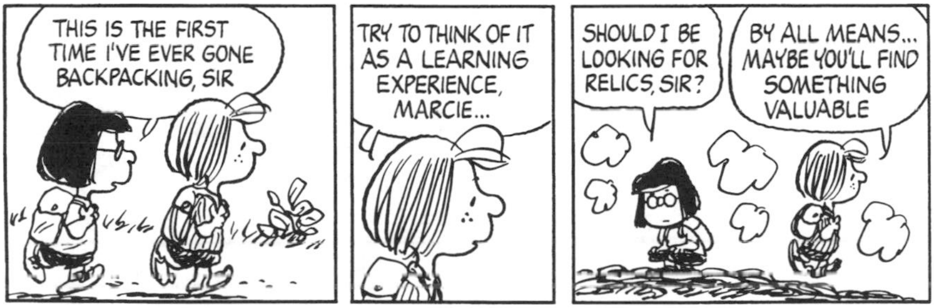
THIS IS THE FIRST TIME I'VE EVER GONE BACKPACKING, SIR
TRY TO THINK OF IT AS A LEARNING EXPERIENCE, MARCIE...
SHOULD I BE LOOKING FOR RELICS, SIR?
BY ALL MEANS... MAYBE YOU'LL FIND SOMETHING VALUABLE

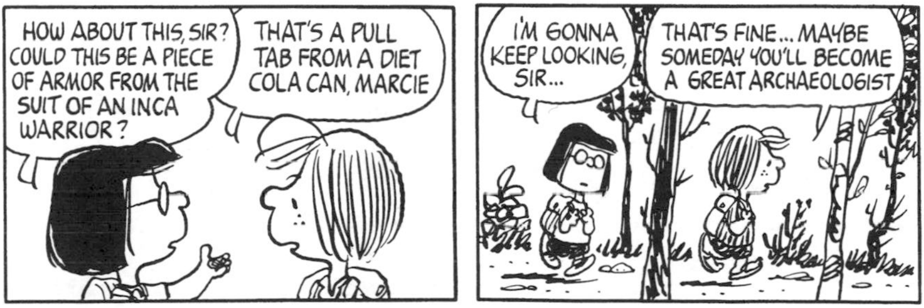
HOW ABOUT THIS, SIR? COULD THIS BE A PIECE OF ARMOR FROM THE SUIT OF AN INCA WARRIOR?
THAT'S A PULL TAB FROM A DIET COLA CAN, MARCIE
I'M GONNA KEEP LOOKING, SIR...
THAT'S FINE... MAYBE SOMEDAY YOU'LL BECOME A GREAT ARCHAEOLOGIST

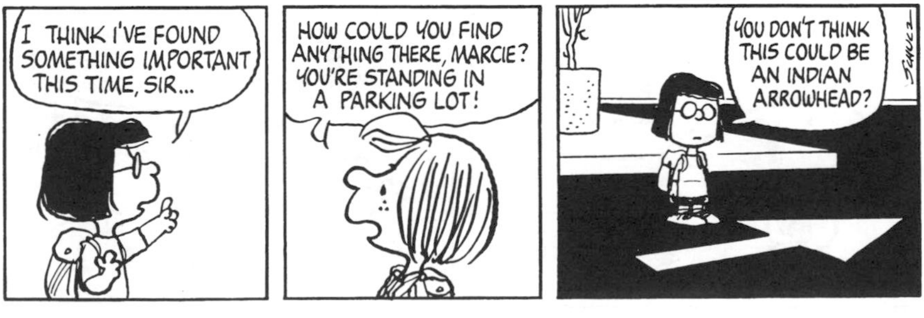
I THINK I'VE FOUND SOMETHING IMPORTANT THIS TIME, SIR...
HOW COULD YOU FIND ANYTHING THERE, MARCIE? YOU'RE STANDING IN A PARKING LOT!
YOU DON'T THINK THIS COULD BE AN INDIAN ARROWHEAD?

OKAY, MEN! RISE AND SHINE!

LET'S CHOW DOWN, AND GET READY TO HIT THE TRAIL

I KNOW EVERYONE IS TIRED, BUT WE HAVE A LOT OF GROUND TO COVER TODAY...

WHERE'S OLIVIER? HE'S FALLEN BEHIND AGAIN...

WE'LL TRAVEL A WHOLE LOT FASTER, OLIVIER, IF YOU'LL GET OUT OF YOUR SLEEPING BAG!

SCHULZ

I SUPPOSE WE SHOULD BE OBSERVING WILDLIFE WHILE WE'RE OUT HERE, SHOULDN'T WE, SIR?

ABSOLUTELY, MARCIE.. THAT'S ONE OF THE PURPOSES OF BACKPACKING

?

LOOK, SIR, I THINK I'VE FOUND A STRANGE CREATURE...IT LOOKS LIKE A GIANT WORM OR SOMETHING...

THAT'S A BIRD IN A SLEEPING BAG, MARCIE! YOU'VE FOUND A BIRD IN A SLEEPING BAG!

I THINK WE'VE DISTURBED THE WILDLIFE, SIR, OR UPSET THE BALANCE OF NATURE OR SOMETHING...

A BIRD IN A SLEEPING BAG?!

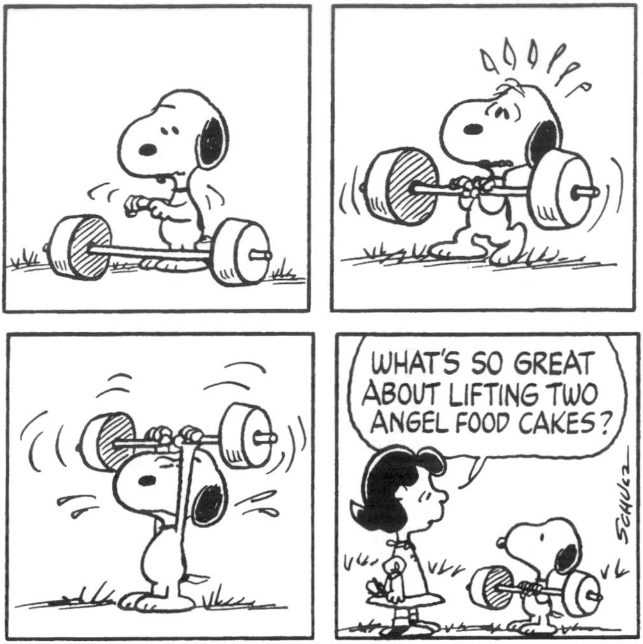
WHAT'S SO GREAT ABOUT LIFTING TWO ANGEL FOOD CAKES?
SCHULZ

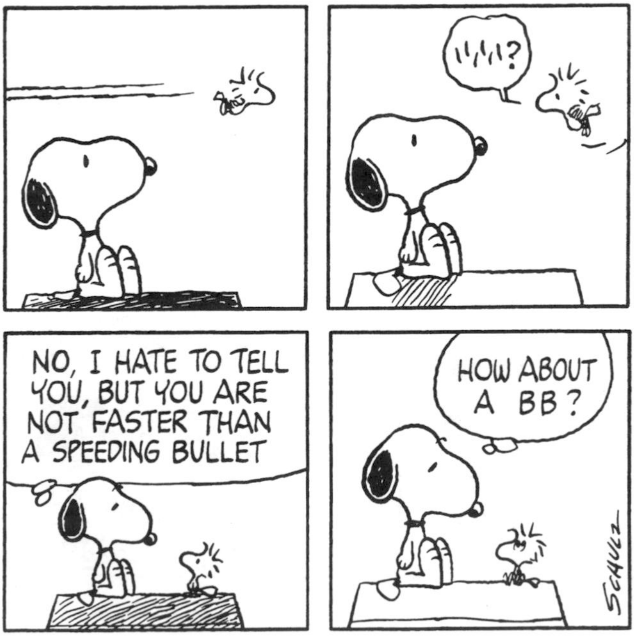
NO, I HATE TO TELL YOU, BUT YOU ARE NOT FASTER THAN A SPEEDING BULLET
HOW ABOUT A BB?
SCHULZ

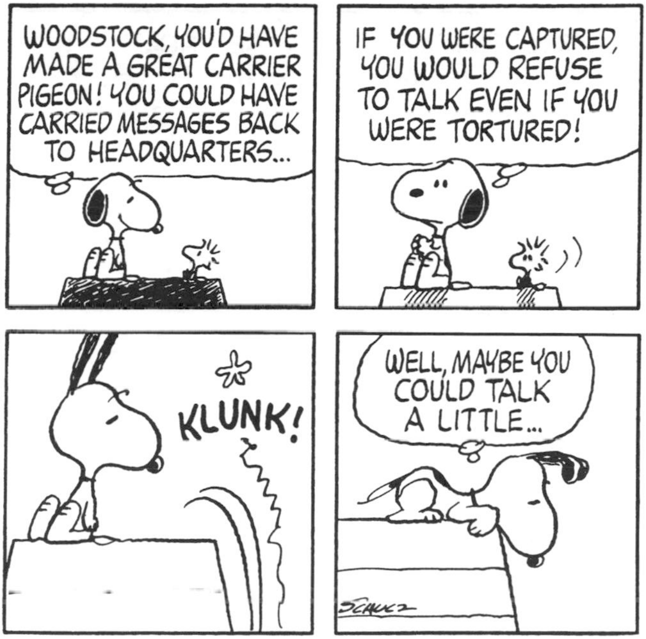
WOODSTOCK, YOU'D HAVE MADE A GREAT CARRIER PIGEON! YOU COULD HAVE CARRIED MESSAGES BACK TO HEADQUARTERS...
IF YOU WERE CAPTURED, YOU WOULD REFUSE TO TALK EVEN IF YOU WERE TORTURED!
KLUNK!
WELL, MAYBE YOU COULD TALK A LITTLE...
SCHULZ

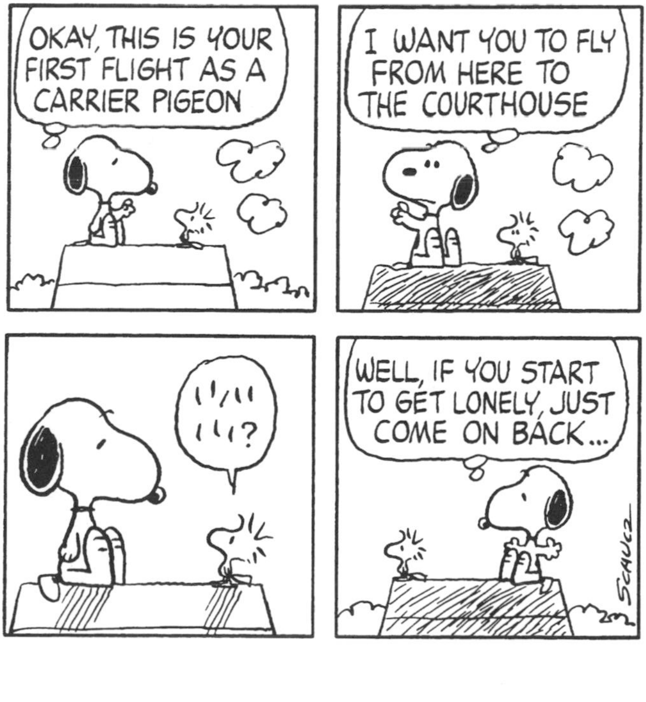
OKAY, THIS IS YOUR FIRST FLIGHT AS A CARRIER PIGEON
I WANT YOU TO FLY FROM HERE TO THE COURTHOUSE
WELL, IF YOU START TO GET LONELY, JUST COME ON BACK...
SCHULZ

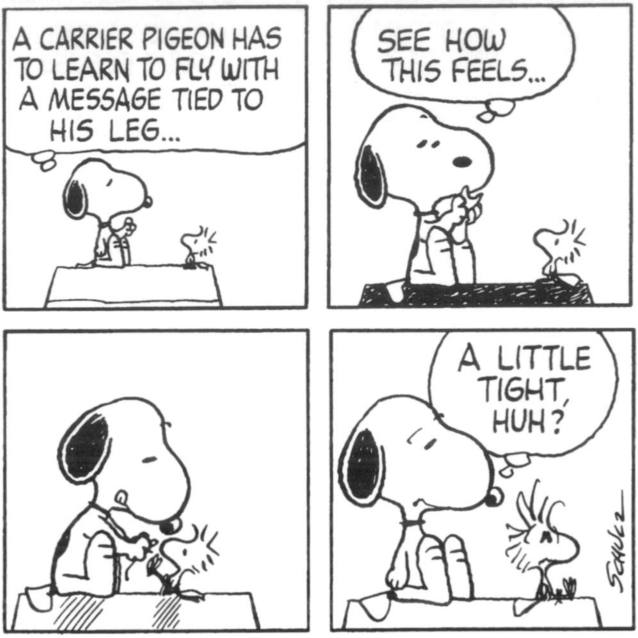
A CARRIER PIGEON HAS TO LEARN TO FLY WITH A MESSAGE TIED TO HIS LEG...
SEE HOW THIS FEELS...
A LITTLE TIGHT, HUH?
SCHULZ

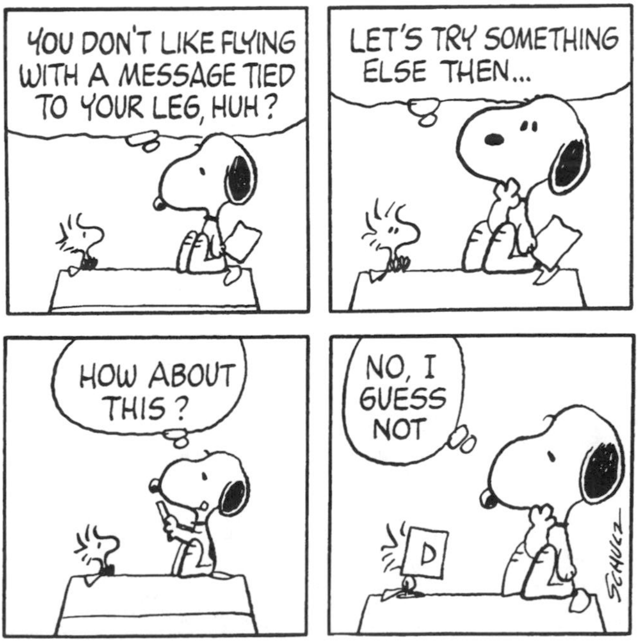
YOU DON'T LIKE FLYING WITH A MESSAGE TIED TO YOUR LEG, HUH?
LET'S TRY SOMETHING ELSE THEN...
HOW ABOUT THIS?
NO, I GUESS NOT
D
SCHULZ

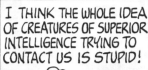

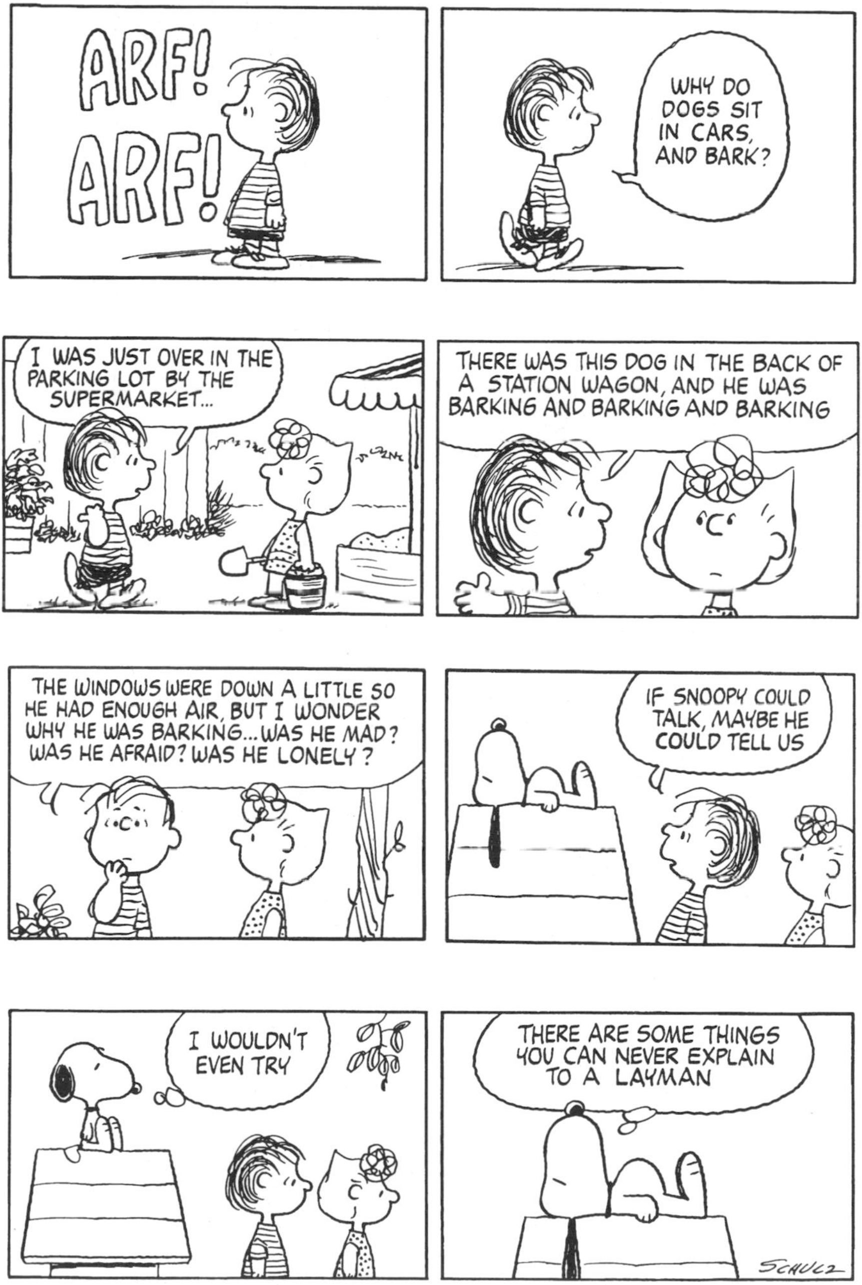
ARF! ARF!
WHY DO DOGS SIT IN CARS, AND BARK?
I WAS JUST OVER IN THE PARKING LOT BY THE SUPERMARKET...
THERE WAS THIS DOG IN THE BACK OF A STATION WAGON, AND HE WAS BARKING AND BARKING AND BARKING
THE WINDOWS WERE DOWN A LITTLE SO HE HAD ENOUGH AIR, BUT I WONDER WHY HE WAS BARKING...WAS HE MAD? WAS HE AFRAID? WAS HE LONELY?
IF SNOOPY COULD TALK, MAYBE HE COULD TELL US
I WOULDN'T EVEN TRY
THERE ARE SOME THINGS YOU CAN NEVER EXPLAIN TO A LAYMAN
SCHULZ

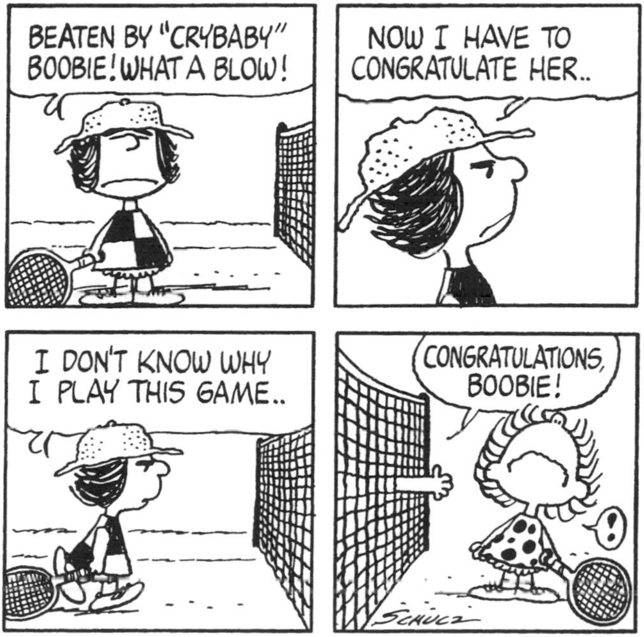
BEATEN BY "CRYBABY" BOOBIE! WHAT A BLOW!
NOW I HAVE TO CONGRATULATE HER..
I DON'T KNOW WHY I PLAY THIS GAME..
CONGRATULATIONS, BOOBIE!
!
SCHULZ

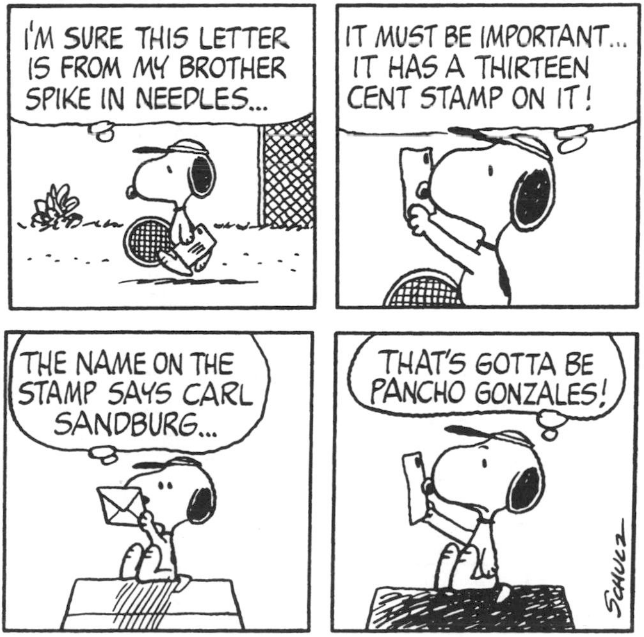
I'M SURE THIS LETTER IS FROM MY BROTHER SPIKE IN NEEDLES...
IT MUST BE IMPORTANT... IT HAS A THIRTEEN CENT STAMP ON IT!
THE NAME ON THE STAMP SAYS CARL SANDBURG...
THAT'S GOTTA BE PANCHO GONZALES!
SCHULZ

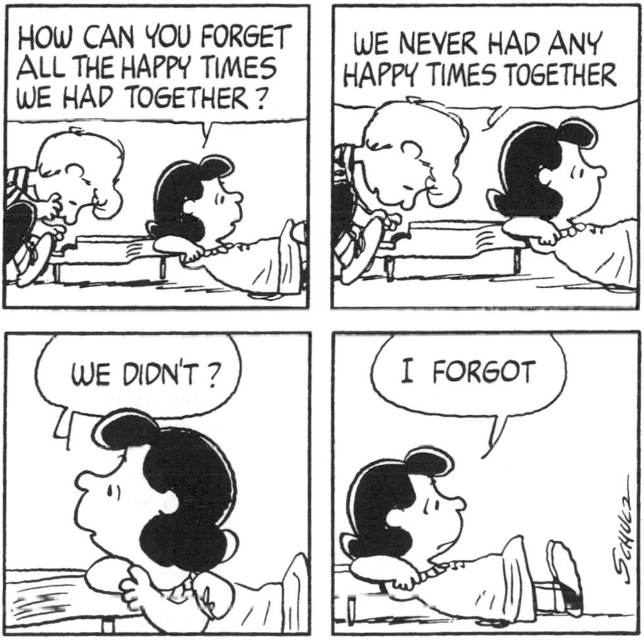
HOW CAN YOU FORGET ALL THE HAPPY TIMES WE HAD TOGETHER?
WE NEVER HAD ANY HAPPY TIMES TOGETHER
WE DIDN'T?
I FORGOT
SCHULZ

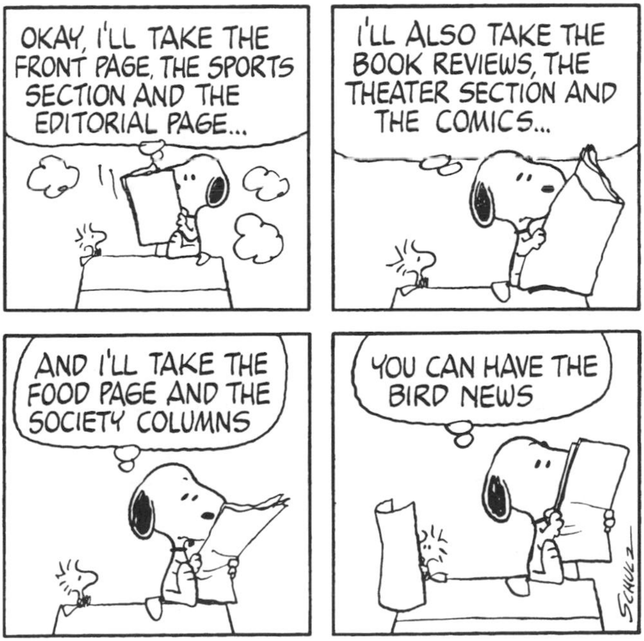
OKAY, I'LL TAKE THE FRONT PAGE, THE SPORTS SECTION AND THE EDITORIAL PAGE...
I'LL ALSO TAKE THE BOOK REVIEWS, THE THEATER SECTION AND THE COMICS...
AND I'LL TAKE THE FOOD PAGE AND THE SOCIETY COLUMNS
YOU CAN HAVE THE BIRD NEWS
SCHULZ

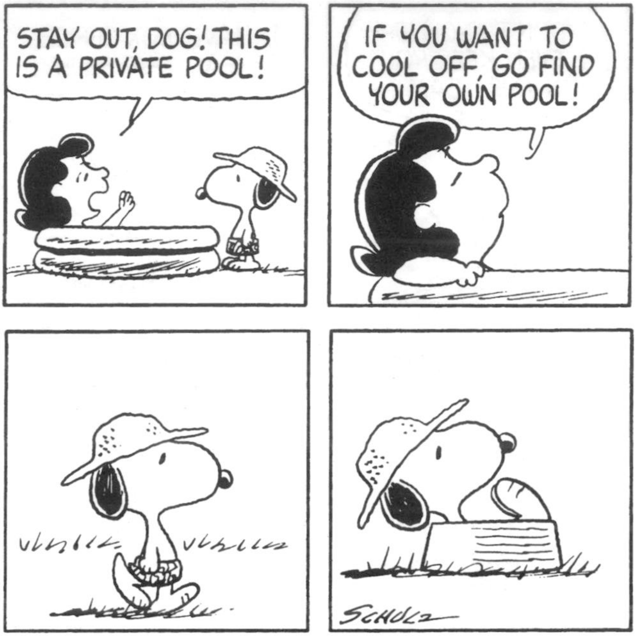
STAY OUT, DOG! THIS IS A PRIVATE POOL!
IF YOU WANT TO COOL OFF, GO FIND YOUR OWN POOL!
SCHULZ

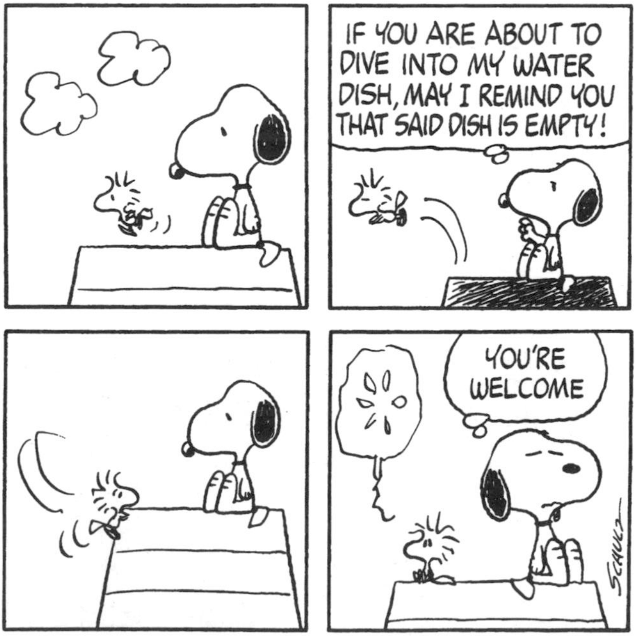
IF YOU ARE ABOUT TO DIVE INTO MY WATER DISH, MAY I REMIND YOU THAT SAID DISH IS EMPTY!
YOU'RE WELCOME
SCHULZ

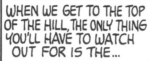

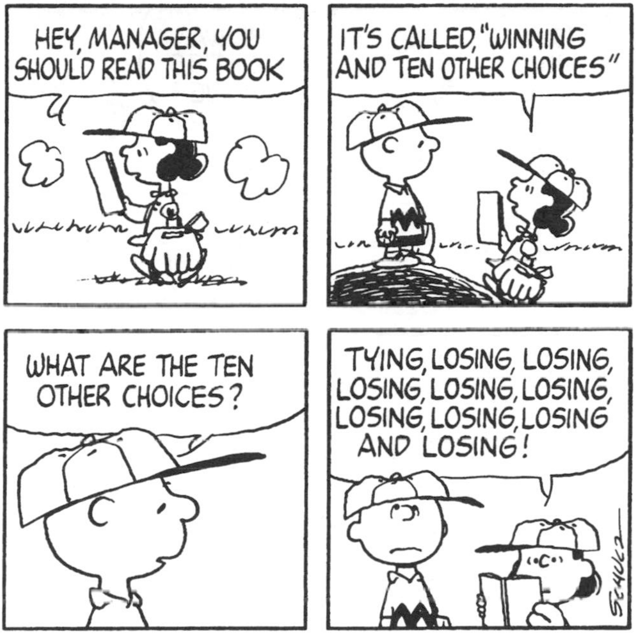
HEY, MANAGER, YOU SHOULD READ THIS BOOK
IT'S CALLED, "WINNING AND TEN OTHER CHOICES"
WHAT ARE THE TEN OTHER CHOICES?
TYING, LOSING, LOSING, LOSING, LOSING, LOSING, LOSING, LOSING, LOSING AND LOSING!
SCHULZ

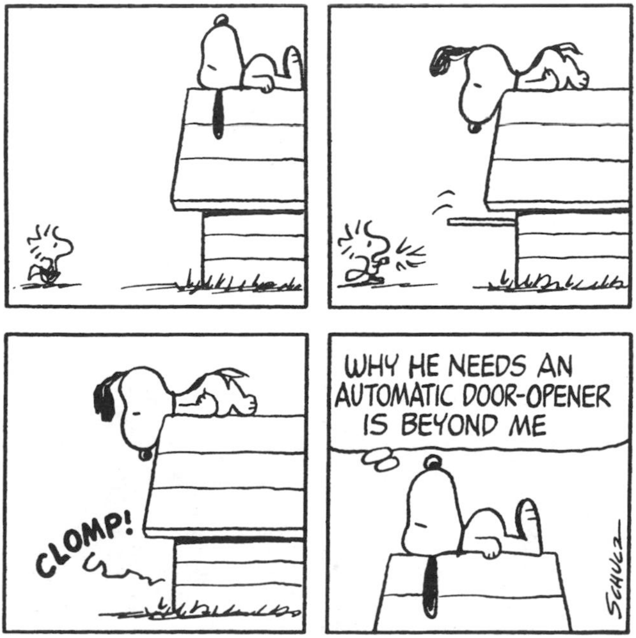
CLOMP!
WHY HE NEEDS AN AUTOMATIC DOOR-OPENER IS BEYOND ME
SCHULZ

KING TIGLATH-PILESER OF ASSYRIA CONQUERED MANY NATIONS, AND CARRIED OFF THEIR BOOTY

THIS MEANT THAT NONE OF THE LITTLE BABIES HAD ANY BOOTIES

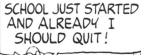

HAHAHAHA HA HA

IF IT HAD HAPPENED TO YOU, MAYBE YOU WOULDN'T BE LAUGHING!

SCHULZ

SCHOOL JUST STARTED AND ALREADY I SHOULD QUIT!

MY TEACHER YELLS AT ME, THE KIDS LAUGH AT ME AND THE PRINCIPAL HATES ME

WHAT ABOUT THE CUSTODIAN?

SCHULZ

HE VACUUMED UP MY LUNCH!

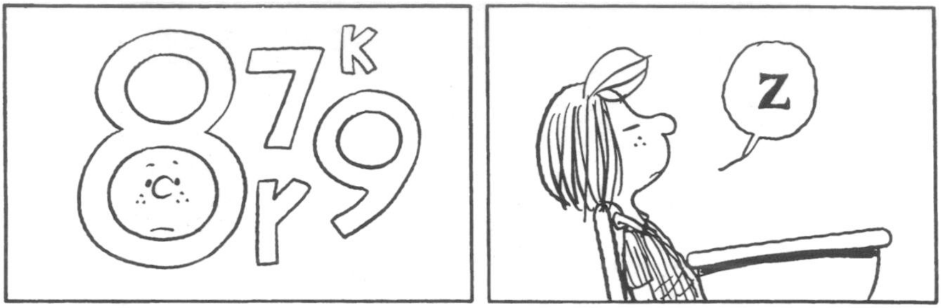
Z

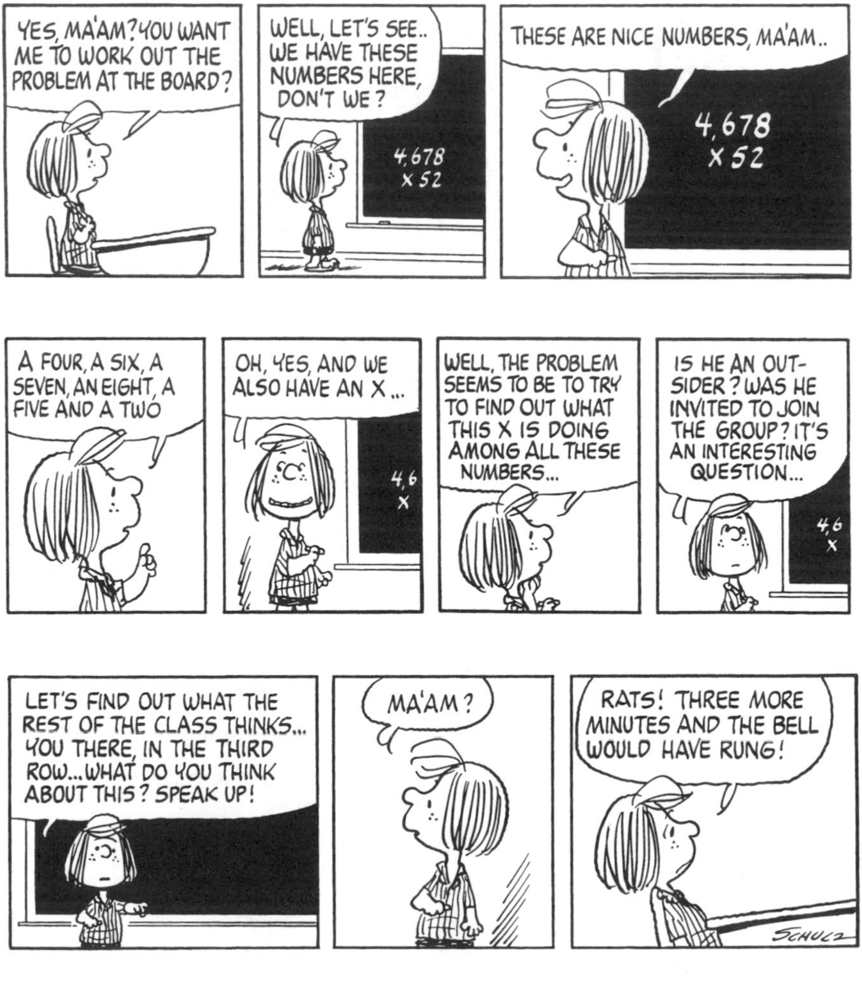
YES, MA'AM? YOU WANT ME TO WORK OUT THE PROBLEM AT THE BOARD?
WELL, LET'S SEE.. WE HAVE THESE NUMBERS HERE, DON'T WE?
4,678
X 52
THESE ARE NICE NUMBERS, MA'AM..
4,678
X 52
A FOUR, A SIX, A SEVEN, AN EIGHT, A FIVE AND A TWO
OH, YES, AND WE ALSO HAVE AN X...
WELL, THE PROBLEM SEEMS TO BE TO TRY TO FIND OUT WHAT THIS X IS DOING AMONG ALL THESE NUMBERS...
IS HE AN OUT-SIDER? WAS HE INVITED TO JOIN THE GROUP? IT'S AN INTERESTING QUESTION...
LET'S FIND OUT WHAT THE REST OF THE CLASS THINKS... YOU THERE, IN THE THIRD ROW...WHAT DO YOU THINK ABOUT THIS? SPEAK UP!
MA'AM?
RATS! THREE MORE MINUTES AND THE BELL WOULD HAVE RUNG!
SCHULZ

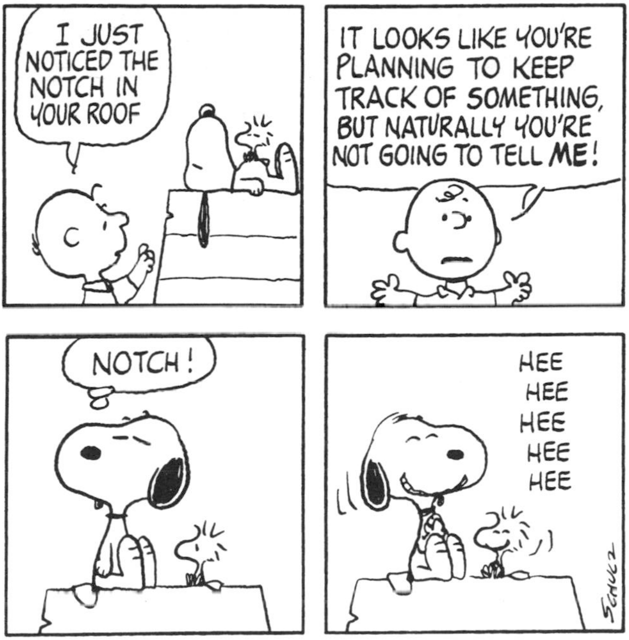
I JUST NOTICED THE NOTCH IN YOUR ROOF
IT LOOKS LIKE YOU'RE PLANNING TO KEEP TRACK OF SOMETHING, BUT NATURALLY YOU'RE NOT GOING TO TELL ME!
NOTCH!
HEE HEE HEE HEE HEE

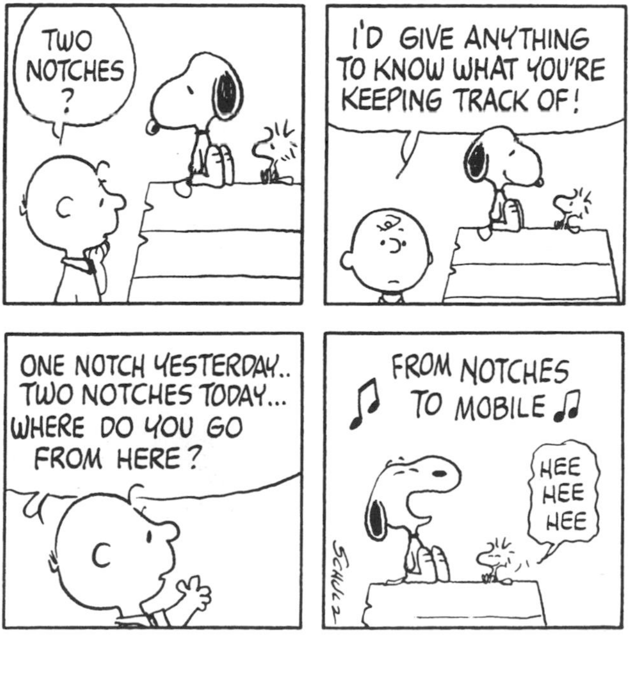
TWO NOTCHES?
I'D GIVE ANYTHING TO KNOW WHAT YOU'RE KEEPING TRACK OF!
ONE NOTCH YESTERDAY.. TWO NOTCHES TODAY... WHERE DO YOU GO FROM HERE?
FROM NOTCHES TO MOBILE
HEE HEE HEE

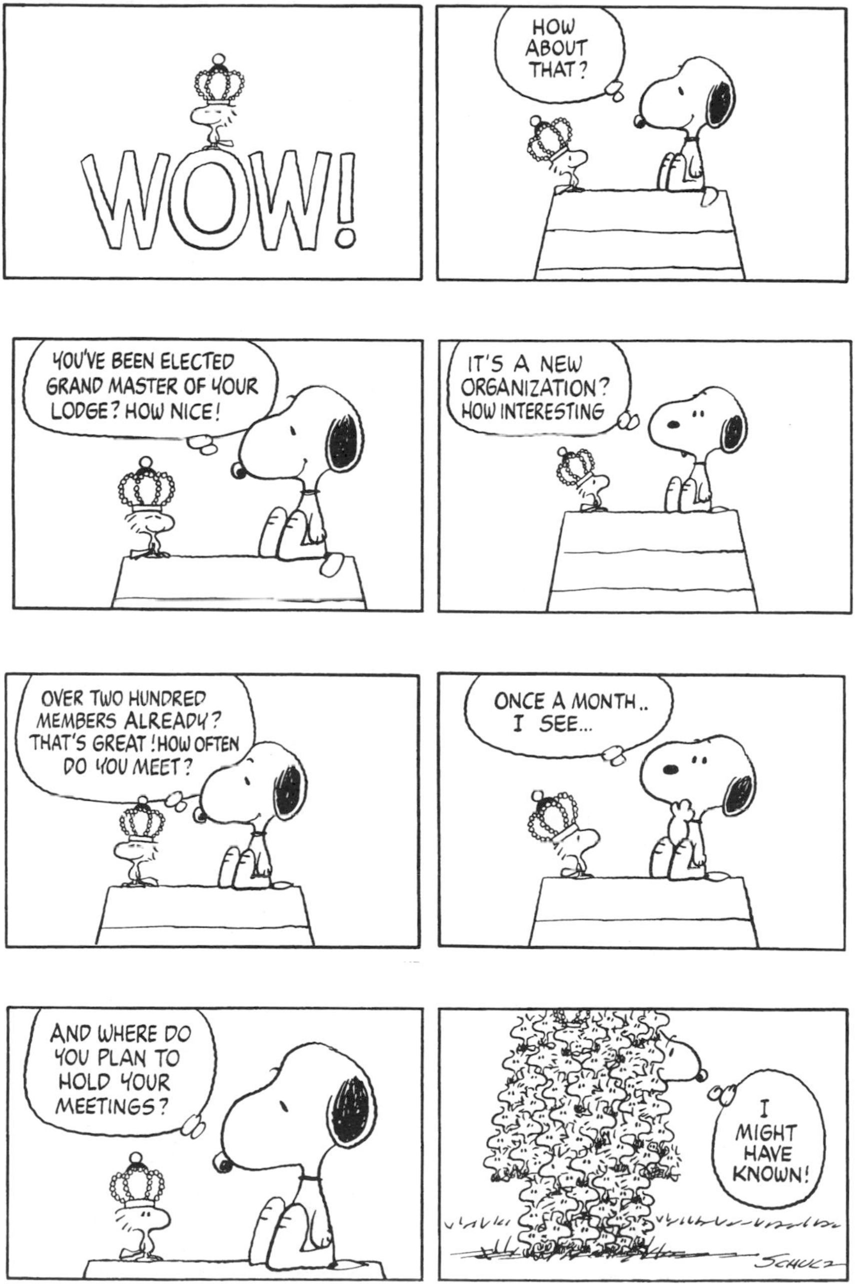
WOW!
HOW ABOUT THAT?
YOU'VE BEEN ELECTED GRAND MASTER OF YOUR LODGE? HOW NICE!
IT'S A NEW ORGANIZATION? HOW INTERESTING
OVER TWO HUNDRED MEMBERS ALREADY? THAT'S GREAT! HOW OFTEN DO YOU MEET?
ONCE A MONTH.. I SEE...
AND WHERE DO YOU PLAN TO HOLD YOUR MEETINGS?
I MIGHT HAVE KNOWN!
SCHULZ

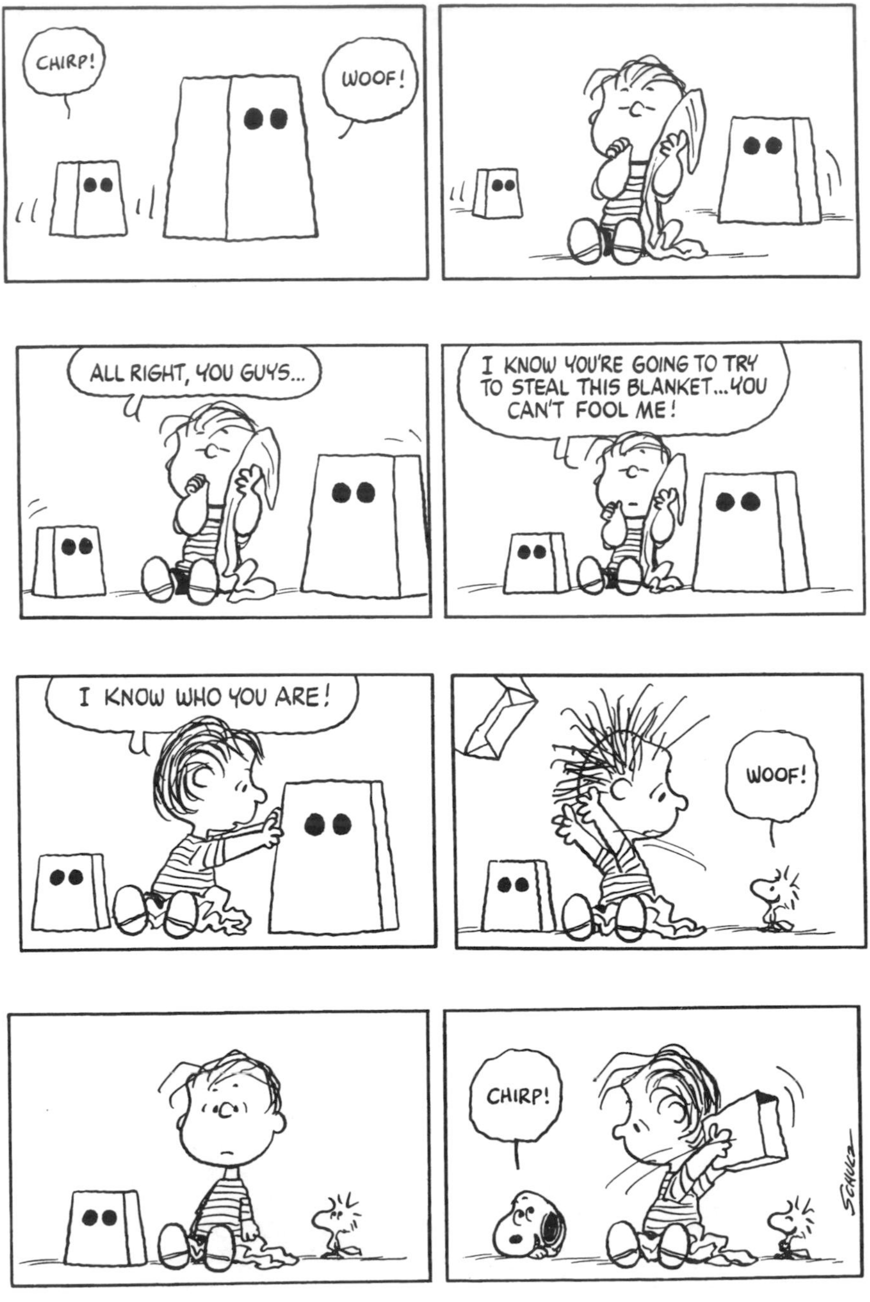
CHIRP!
WOOF!
ALL RIGHT, YOU GUYS...
I KNOW YOU'RE GOING TO TRY TO STEAL THIS BLANKET...YOU CAN'T FOOL ME!
I KNOW WHO YOU ARE!
WOOF!
CHIRP!
SCHULZ

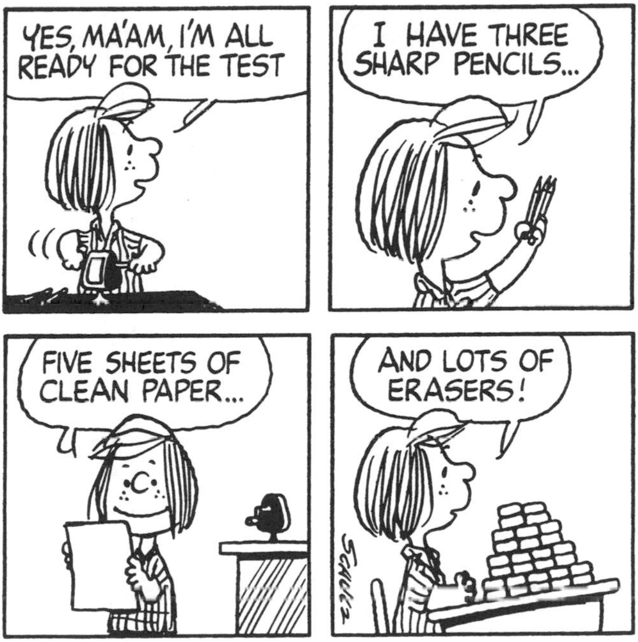
YES, MA'AM, I'M ALL READY FOR THE TEST
I HAVE THREE SHARP PENCILS...
FIVE SHEETS OF CLEAN PAPER...
AND LOTS OF ERASERS!

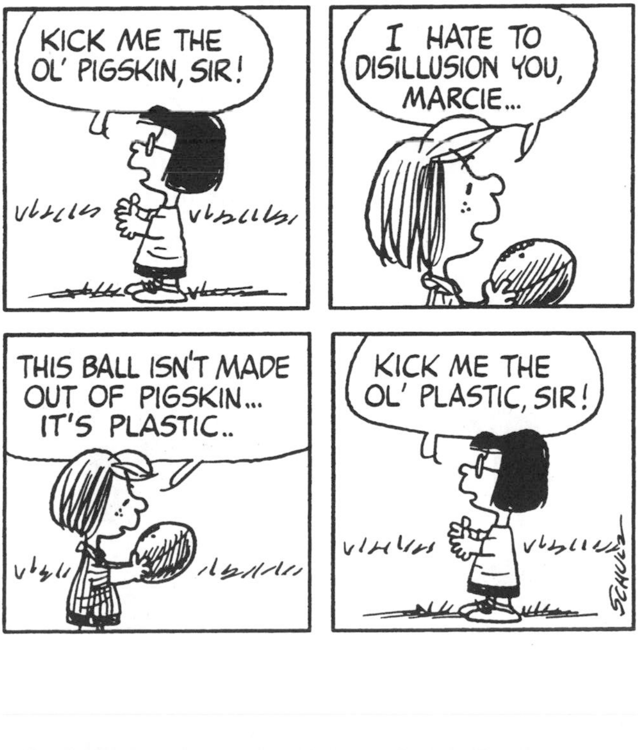
KICK ME THE OL' PIGSKIN, SIR!
I HATE TO DISILLUSION YOU, MARCIE...
THIS BALL ISN'T MADE OUT OF PIGSKIN... IT'S PLASTIC..
KICK ME THE OL' PLASTIC, SIR!

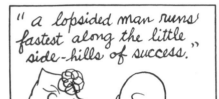

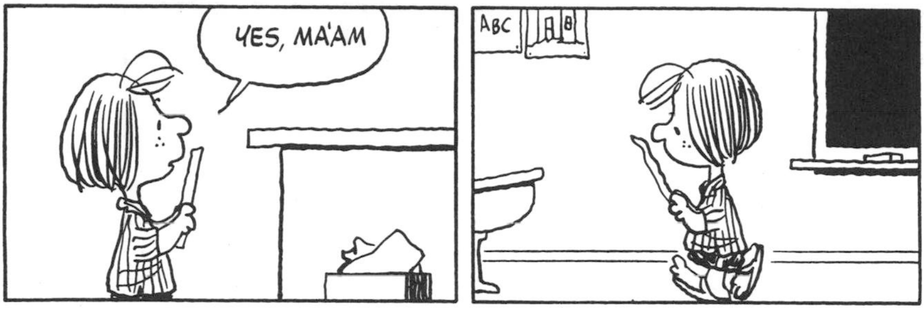
YES, MA'AM
ABC

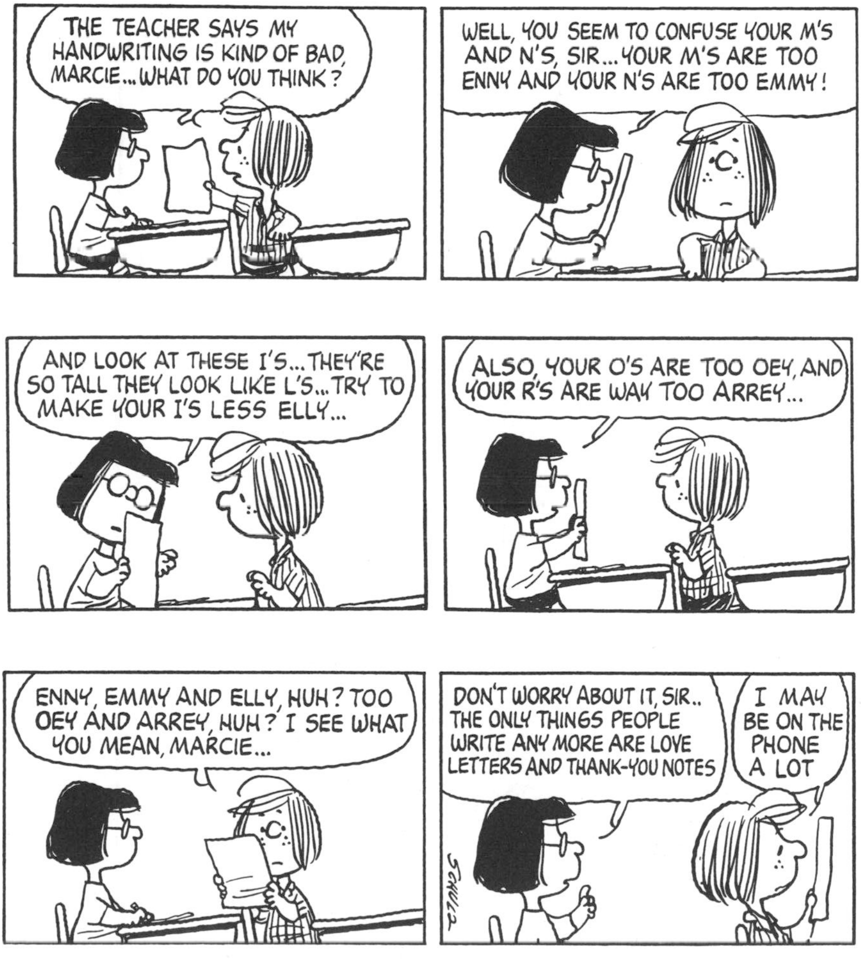
THE TEACHER SAYS MY HANDWRITING IS KIND OF BAD, MARCIE... WHAT DO YOU THINK?
WELL, YOU SEEM TO CONFUSE YOUR M'S AND N'S, SIR... YOUR M'S ARE TOO ENNY AND YOUR N'S ARE TOO EMMY!
AND LOOK AT THESE I'S... THEY'RE SO TALL THEY LOOK LIKE L'S... TRY TO MAKE YOUR I'S LESS ELLY...
ALSO, YOUR O'S ARE TOO OEY, AND YOUR R'S ARE WAY TOO ARREY...
ENNY, EMMY AND ELLY, HUH? TOO OEY AND ARREY, HUH? I SEE WHAT YOU MEAN, MARCIE...
DON'T WORRY ABOUT IT, SIR.. THE ONLY THINGS PEOPLE WRITE ANY MORE ARE LOVE LETTERS AND THANK-YOU NOTES
I MAY BE ON THE PHONE A LOT
SCHULZ

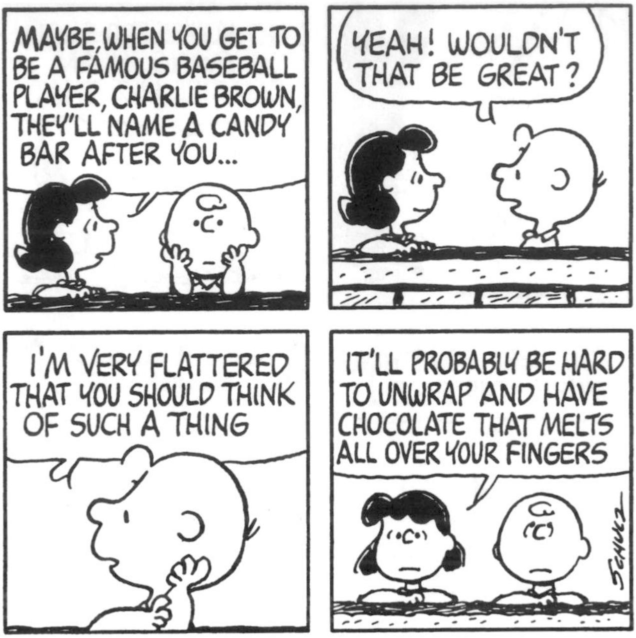
MAYBE, WHEN YOU GET TO BE A FAMOUS BASEBALL PLAYER, CHARLIE BROWN, THEY'LL NAME A CANDY BAR AFTER YOU...
YEAH! WOULDN'T THAT BE GREAT?
I'M VERY FLATTERED THAT YOU SHOULD THINK OF SUCH A THING
IT'LL PROBABLY BE HARD TO UNWRAP AND HAVE CHOCOLATE THAT MELTS ALL OVER YOUR FINGERS
SCHULZ

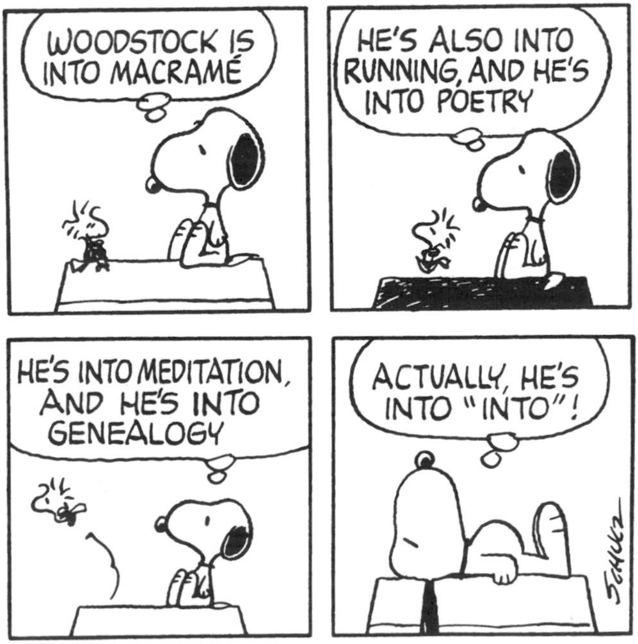
WOODSTOCK IS INTO MACRAMÉ
HE'S ALSO INTO RUNNING, AND HE'S INTO POETRY
HE'S INTO MEDITATION, AND HE'S INTO GENEALOGY
ACTUALLY, HE'S INTO "INTO"!
SCHULZ

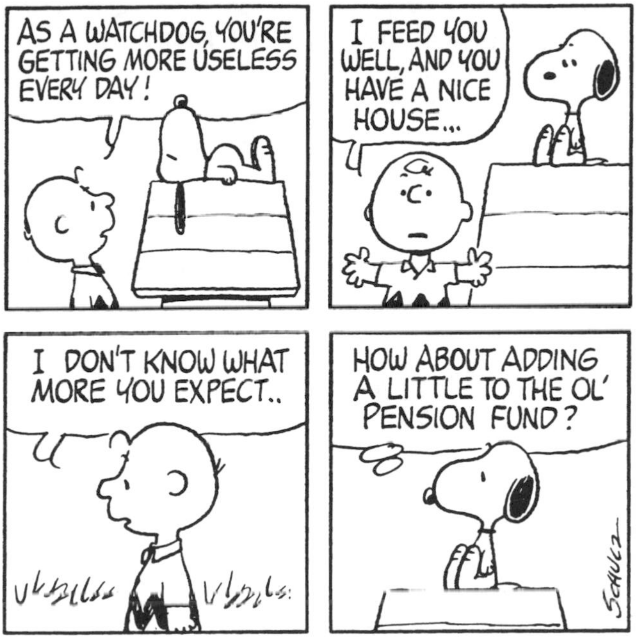
AS A WATCHDOG, YOU'RE GETTING MORE USELESS EVERY DAY!
I FEED YOU WELL, AND YOU HAVE A NICE HOUSE...
I DON'T KNOW WHAT MORE YOU EXPECT..
HOW ABOUT ADDING A LITTLE TO THE OL' PENSION FUND?
SCHULZ

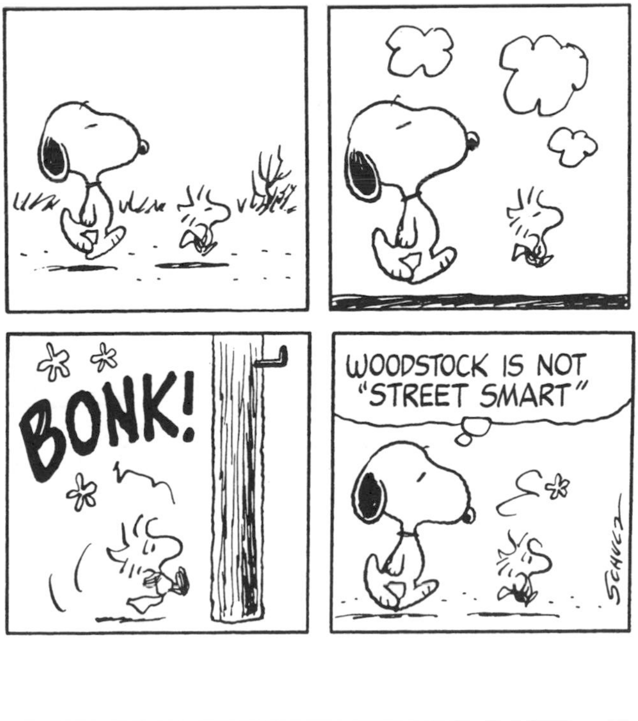
BONK!
WOODSTOCK IS NOT "STREET SMART"
SCHULZ

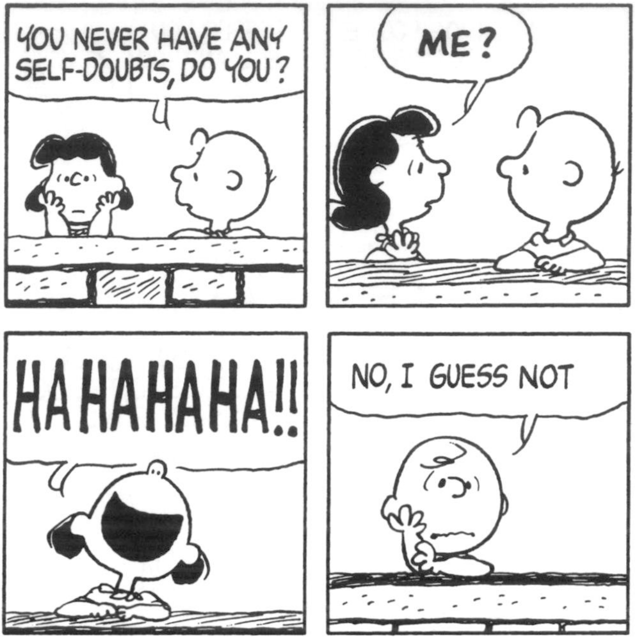
YOU NEVER HAVE ANY SELF-DOUBTS, DO YOU?
ME?
HAHAHAHA!!
NO, I GUESS NOT

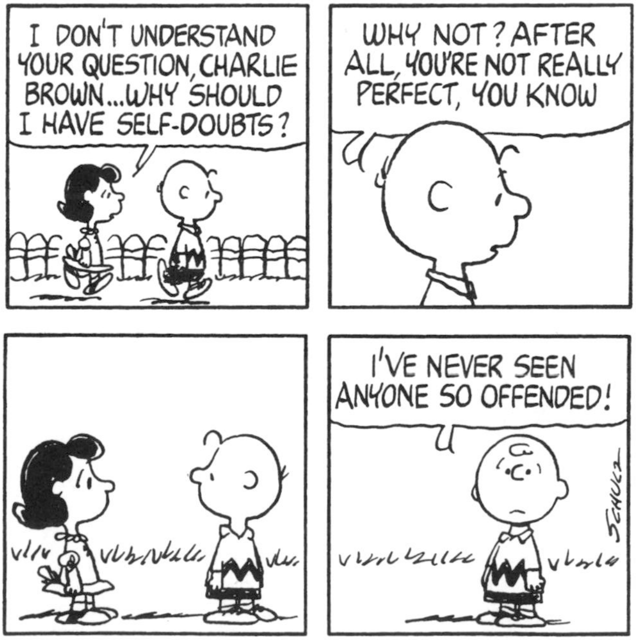
I DON'T UNDERSTAND YOUR QUESTION, CHARLIE BROWN...WHY SHOULD I HAVE SELF-DOUBTS?
WHY NOT? AFTER ALL, YOU'RE NOT REALLY PERFECT, YOU KNOW
I'VE NEVER SEEN ANYONE SO OFFENDED!
SCHULZ

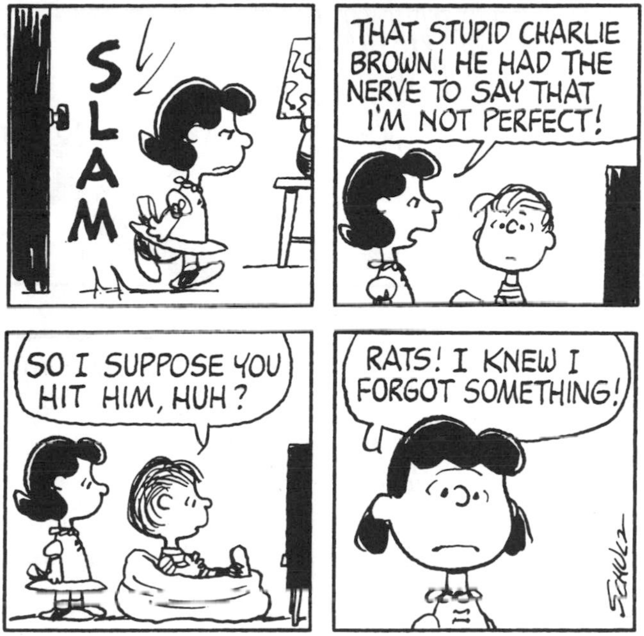
SLAM
THAT STUPID CHARLIE BROWN! HE HAD THE NERVE TO SAY THAT I'M NOT PERFECT!
SO I SUPPOSE YOU HIT HIM, HUH?
RATS! I KNEW I FORGOT SOMETHING!
SCHULZ

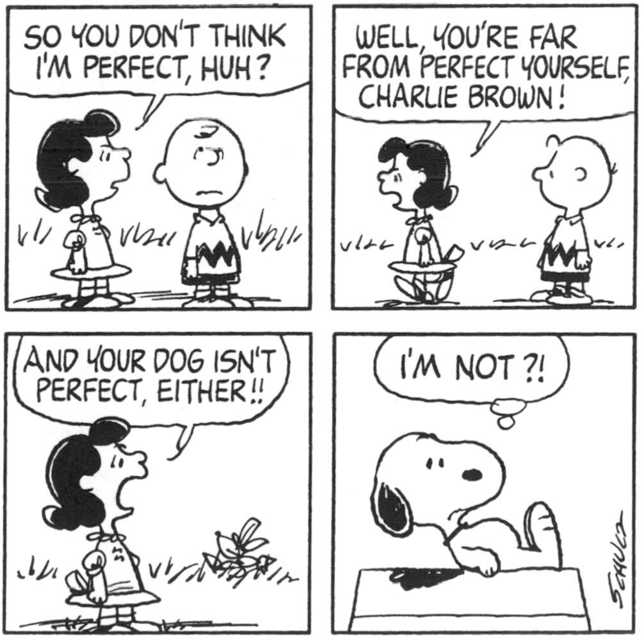
SO YOU DON'T THINK I'M PERFECT, HUH?
WELL, YOU'RE FAR FROM PERFECT YOURSELF, CHARLIE BROWN!
AND YOUR DOG ISN'T PERFECT, EITHER!!
I'M NOT ?!
SCHULZ

LOOK, MEN! IT'S STARTING TO SNOW AGAIN

MAYBE THIS IS A GOOD THING

THIS WILL GIVE US A CHANCE TO SEE IF YOU'VE LEARNED WHAT I'VE TAUGHT YOU...

WHAT'S THE FIRST THING YOU DO WHEN IT BEGINS TO SNOW?

WAIT!! I DON'T WANT YOU TO TELL ME...I WANT YOU TO SHOW ME!

THE WEATHER MAY GET WORSE, MEN

IS ANYONE WORRIED? DO YOU ALL KNOW HOW TO ACT IN A BLIZZARD? DOES ANYONE HAVE A QUESTION ABOUT ANYTHING?

NO, OLIVIER, I DON'T THINK THERE'S A PLACE AROUND HERE WHERE YOU CAN MAIL YOUR POST CARDS

YES, BILL, I'VE MET CHERYL TIEGS...YES, SHE'S VERY NICE..

SHOPPING DAYS? WELL, CONRAD, I'D GUESS THERE ARE ABOUT TWENTY-FOUR MORE SHOPPING DAYS UNTIL CHRISTMAS

ANY MORE QUESTIONS?

NO, WOODSTOCK, I DON'T KNOW WHY YOU'RE STANDING HERE IN A BLIZZARD WITH THESE THREE IDIOTS...

I DIDN'T THINK I WAS EVER GOING TO GET A SENSIBLE QUESTION

SCHULZ

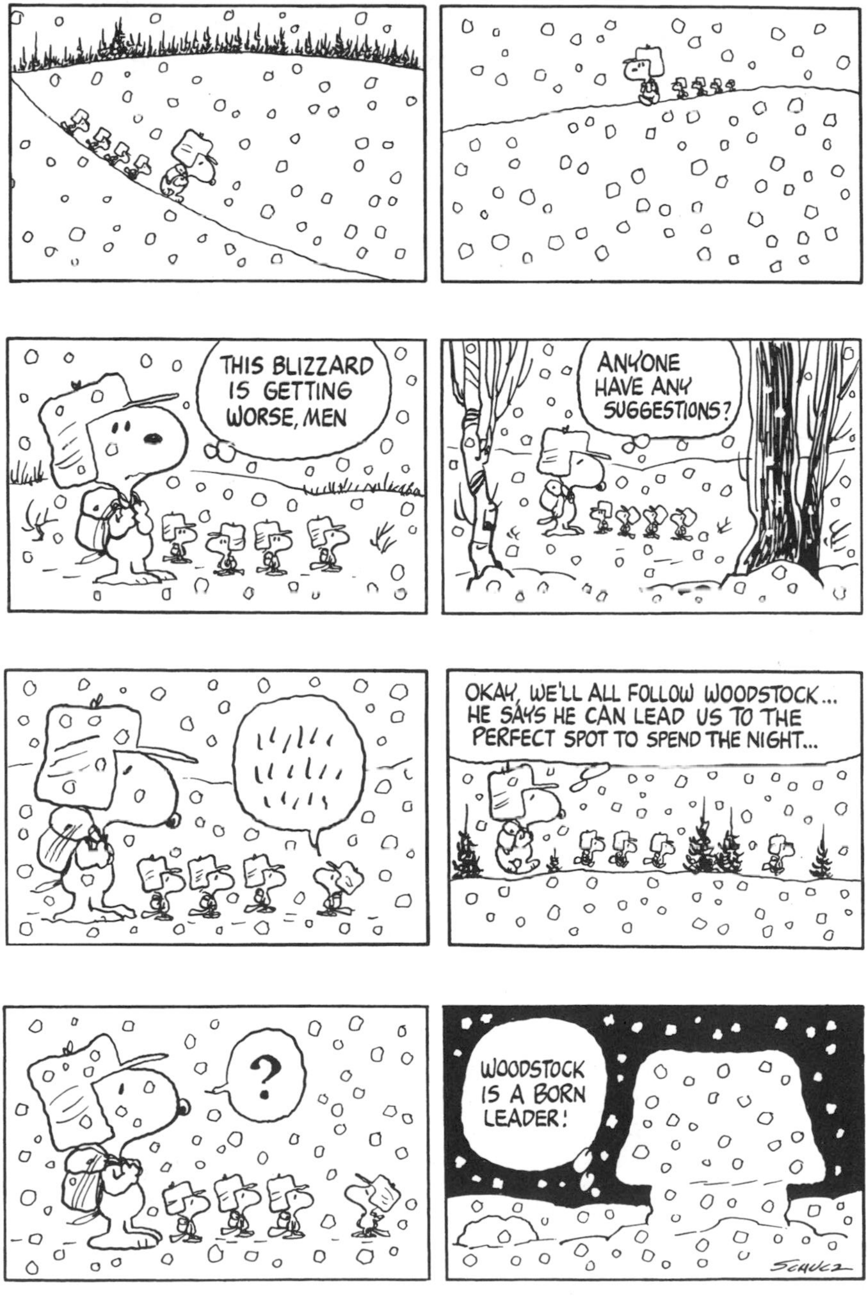
THIS BLIZZARD IS GETTING WORSE, MEN
ANYONE HAVE ANY SUGGESTIONS?
OKAY, WE'LL ALL FOLLOW WOODSTOCK... HE SAYS HE CAN LEAD US TO THE PERFECT SPOT TO SPEND THE NIGHT...
?
WOODSTOCK IS A BORN LEADER!
SCHULZ

IN MY BOOK ABOUT BEETHOVEN, I'VE MADE A FEW IMPROVEMENTS

FOR INSTANCE, INSTEAD OF PLAYING THE PIANO, I HAVE HIM PLAYING AN ELECTRIC GUITAR...

ALSO, IN MY BOOK HE DOESN'T HAVE STOMACH PAINS..

I'VE UPDATED IT TO TENNIS ELBOW!

I HATE TO SHOW ANY INTEREST, BUT IN YOUR BOOK, DOES BEETHOVEN MEET ANY OTHER WOMEN?

OH, YES! IN CHAPTER FOUR HIS LANDLADY SAYS TO HIM, "IF YOU DON'T PAY YOUR RENT, YOU KNOW WHAT I'LL DO?"

"I'LL KICK YOUR PIANO!"

I KNEW I SHOULDN'T HAVE SHOWN ANY INTEREST...

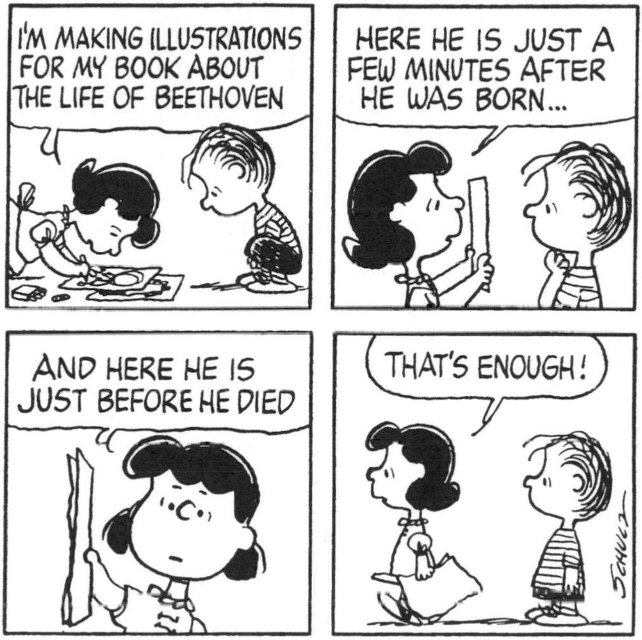
I'M MAKING ILLUSTRATIONS FOR MY BOOK ABOUT THE LIFE OF BEETHOVEN
HERE HE IS JUST A FEW MINUTES AFTER HE WAS BORN...
AND HERE HE IS JUST BEFORE HE DIED
THAT'S ENOUGH!
SCHULZ

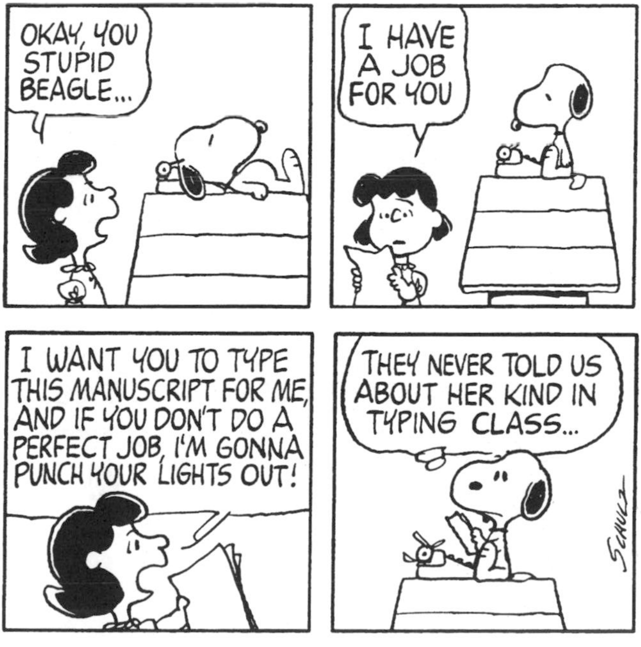
OKAY, YOU STUPID BEAGLE...
I HAVE A JOB FOR YOU
I WANT YOU TO TYPE THIS MANUSCRIPT FOR ME, AND IF YOU DON'T DO A PERFECT JOB, I'M GONNA PUNCH YOUR LIGHTS OUT!
THEY NEVER TOLD US ABOUT HER KIND IN TYPING CLASS...
SCHULZ

A FINE BROTHER YOU ARE! YOU LET ME MAKE A FOOL OUT OF MYSELF!!

IT ISN'T RAIN GEAR! IT'S REINDEER! WHY DIDN'T YOU TELL ME?!

THEY ALL LAUGHED AT ME! EVEN THE TEACHER LAUGHED AT ME! I'LL NEVER BE ABLE TO GO TO THAT SCHOOL AGAIN!

POOR SWEET BABY...

SNIF!

THEY SURE HAD THEIR NERVE LAUGHING AT MY STORY.... HA!

HOW ABOUT THIS THING WITH ALL THE REINDEER PULLING THE SLEIGH THROUGH THE AIR? NO WAY!

I DON'T CARE HOW MANY REINDEER HE HAD, THEY COULD NEVER PRODUCE ENOUGH LIFT TO GET A SLED IN THE AIR...

NO WAY, HUH, BIG BROTHER?

NO WAY! MERRY CHRISTMAS!

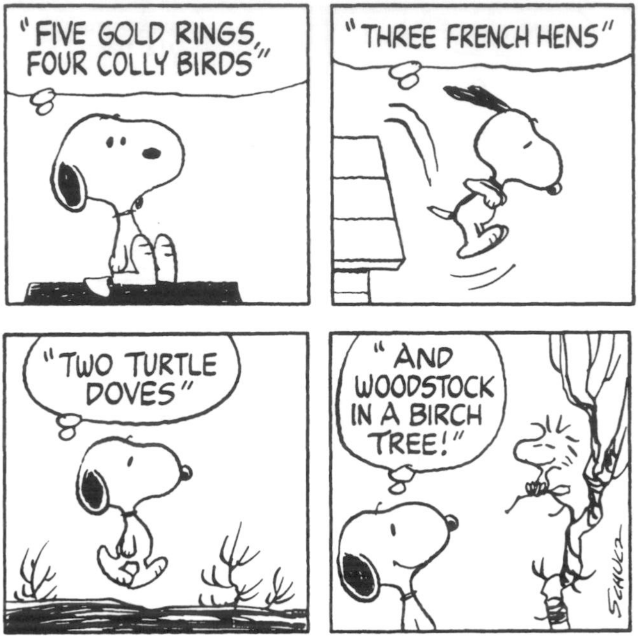
"FIVE GOLD RINGS, FOUR COLLY BIRDS"
"THREE FRENCH HENS"
"TWO TURTLE DOVES"
"AND WOODSTOCK IN A BIRCH TREE!"

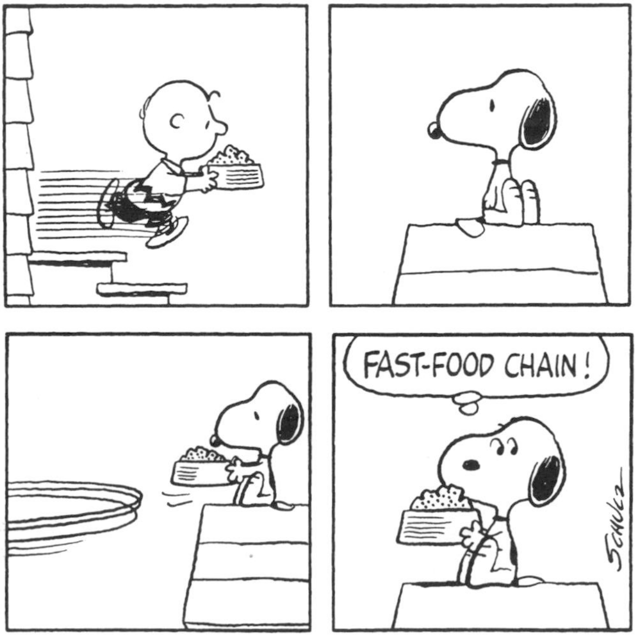
FAST-FOOD CHAIN!

Deer

THAT SHOULD BE "DEAR"

IN THE SALUTATION OF A LETTER, THE PROPER WORD AND SPELLING OF THAT WORD IS "DEAR"

Deer are beautiful animals found in most parts of the world.

I'M SORRY... I DIDN'T REALIZE YOU WERE WRITING ABOUT DEER... I APOLOGIZE...

WELL, I SHOULD HOPE SO! IT SEEMS TO ME THAT A LOT OF THE PROBLEMS IN THIS WORLD ARE CAUSED BY PEOPLE WHO CRITICIZE OTHER PEOPLE BEFORE THEY KNOW WHAT THEY'RE TALKING ABOUT!

Dear Grandma,

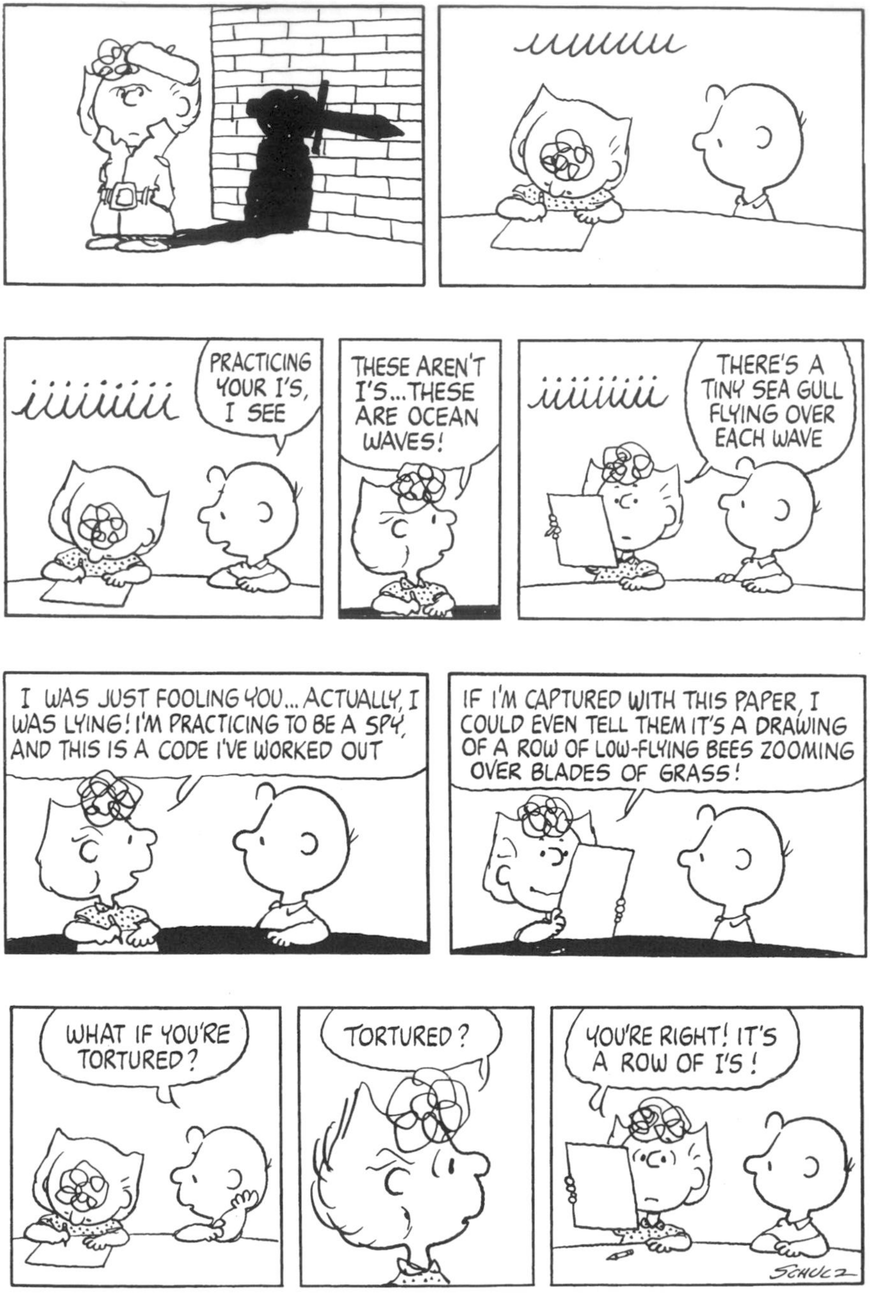

PRACTICING YOUR I'S, I SEE
THESE AREN'T I'S...THESE ARE OCEAN WAVES!
THERE'S A TINY SEA GULL FLYING OVER EACH WAVE
I WAS JUST FOOLING YOU... ACTUALLY, I WAS LYING! I'M PRACTICING TO BE A SPY, AND THIS IS A CODE I'VE WORKED OUT
IF I'M CAPTURED WITH THIS PAPER, I COULD EVEN TELL THEM IT'S A DRAWING OF A ROW OF LOW-FLYING BEES ZOOMING OVER BLADES OF GRASS!
WHAT IF YOU'RE TORTURED?
TORTURED?
YOU'RE RIGHT! IT'S A ROW OF I'S!
SCHULZ

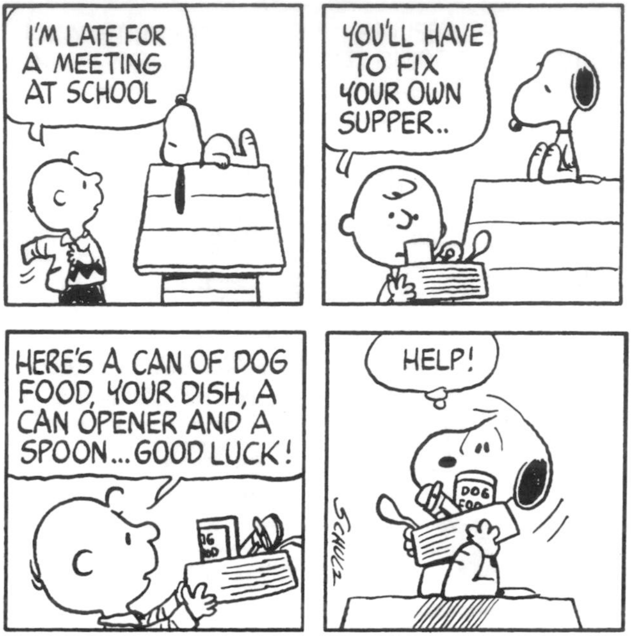
I'M LATE FOR A MEETING AT SCHOOL
YOU'LL HAVE TO FIX YOUR OWN SUPPER..
HERE'S A CAN OF DOG FOOD, YOUR DISH, A CAN OPENER AND A SPOON...GOOD LUCK!
HELP!

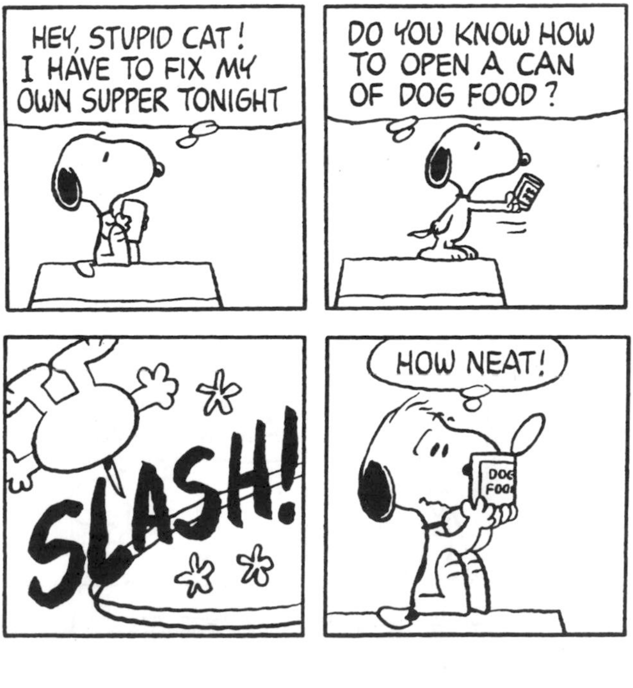
HEY, STUPID CAT! I HAVE TO FIX MY OWN SUPPER TONIGHT
DO YOU KNOW HOW TO OPEN A CAN OF DOG FOOD?
SLASH!
HOW NEAT!

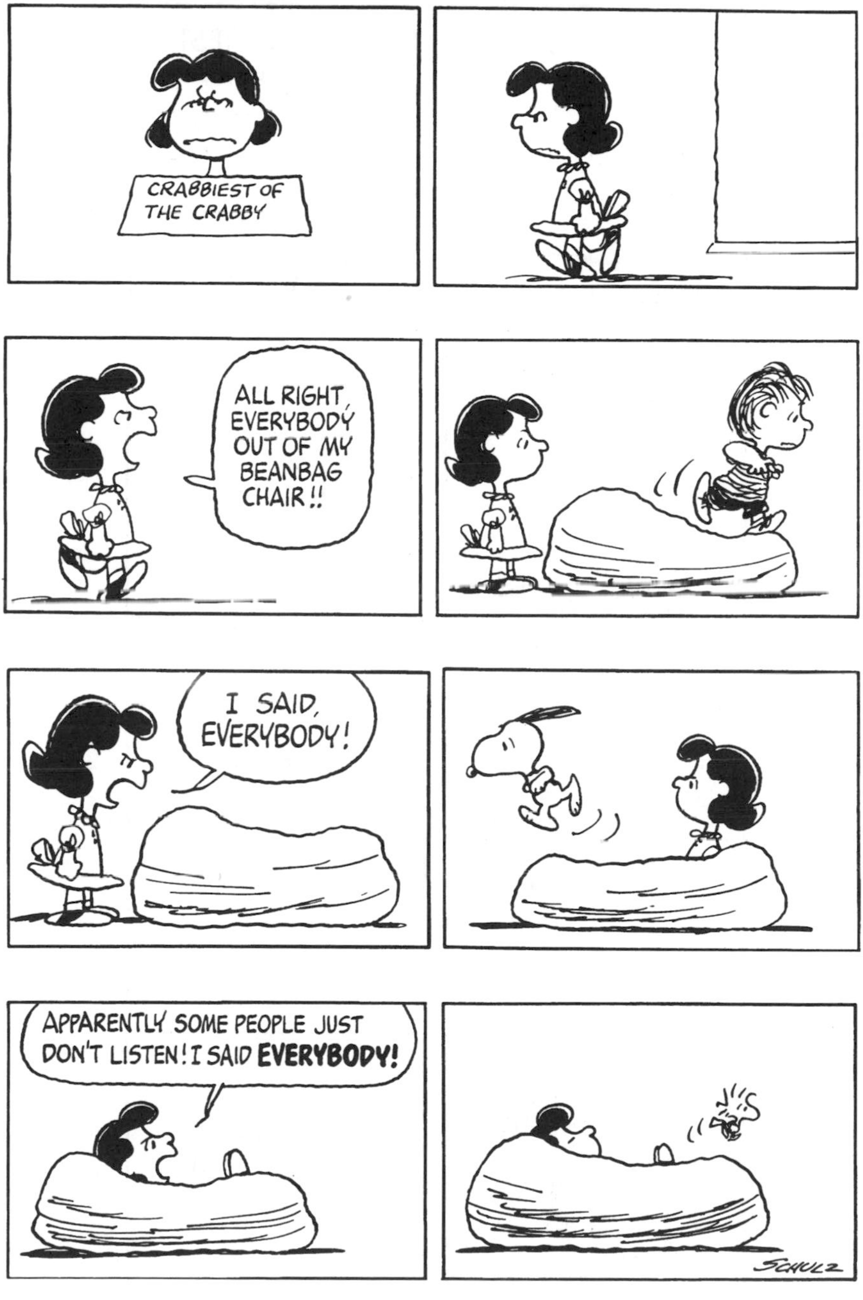
CRABBIEST OF THE CRABBY
ALL RIGHT, EVERYBODY OUT OF MY BEANBAG CHAIR!!
I SAID, EVERYBODY!
APPARENTLY SOME PEOPLE JUST DON'T LISTEN! I SAID **EVERYBODY!**
SCHULZ

IT'S HARD TO CHEER UP A DEPRESSED BIRD

YOU NEED A GIRL FRIEND, THAT'S WHAT YOU NEED

WHY DON'T YOU GO HANG AROUND SOME TELEPHONE WIRES? OR BETTER YET, JOIN A WORM GROUP!

A WORM GROUP! THAT'S A GOOD ONE! HEE HEE HEE HEE HEE!

I'M SORRY! HEE HEE HEE HEE! I ALWAYS LAUGH! HEE HEE HEE!

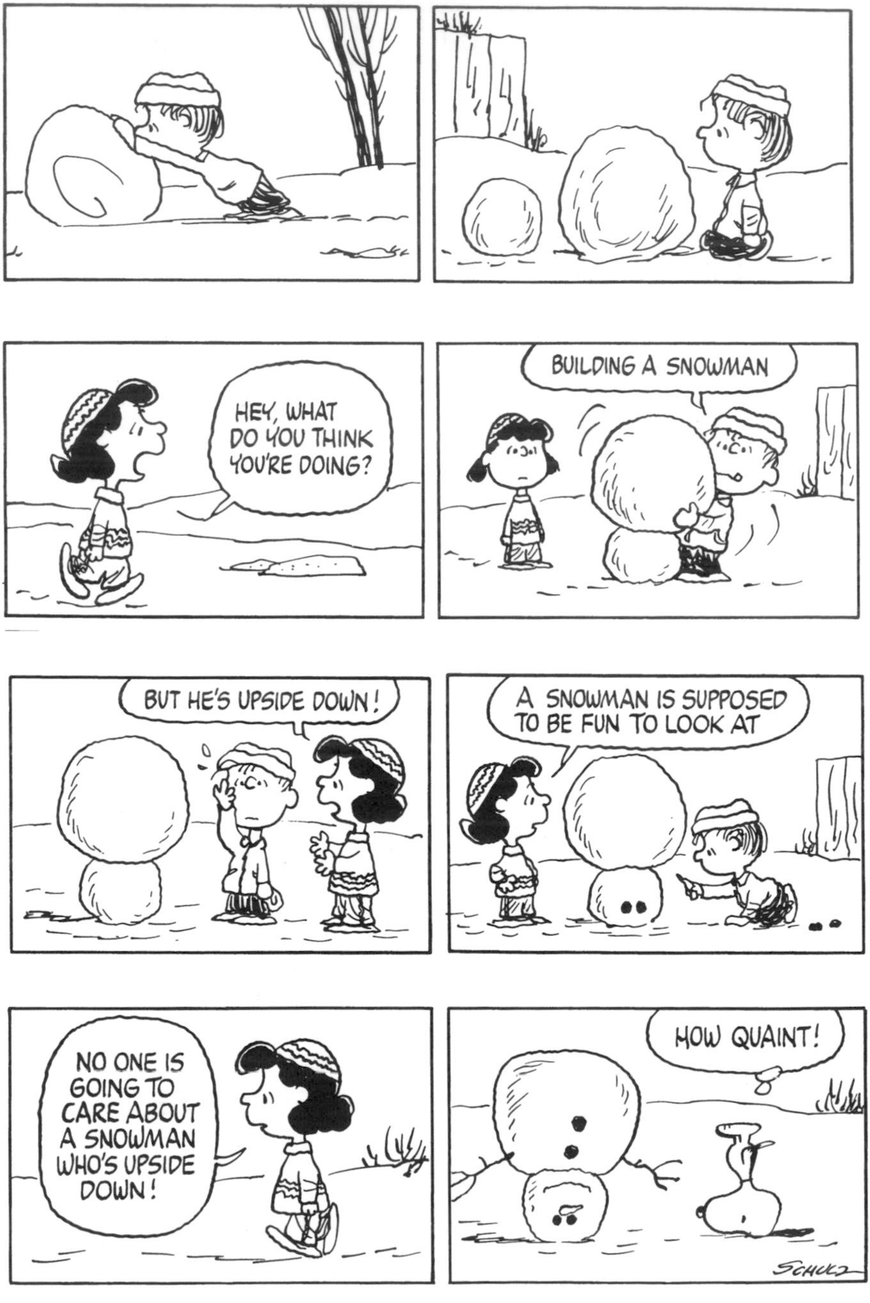
HEY, WHAT DO YOU THINK YOU'RE DOING?
BUILDING A SNOWMAN
BUT HE'S UPSIDE DOWN!
A SNOWMAN IS SUPPOSED TO BE FUN TO LOOK AT
NO ONE IS GOING TO CARE ABOUT A SNOWMAN WHO'S UPSIDE DOWN!
HOW QUAINT!
SCHULZ

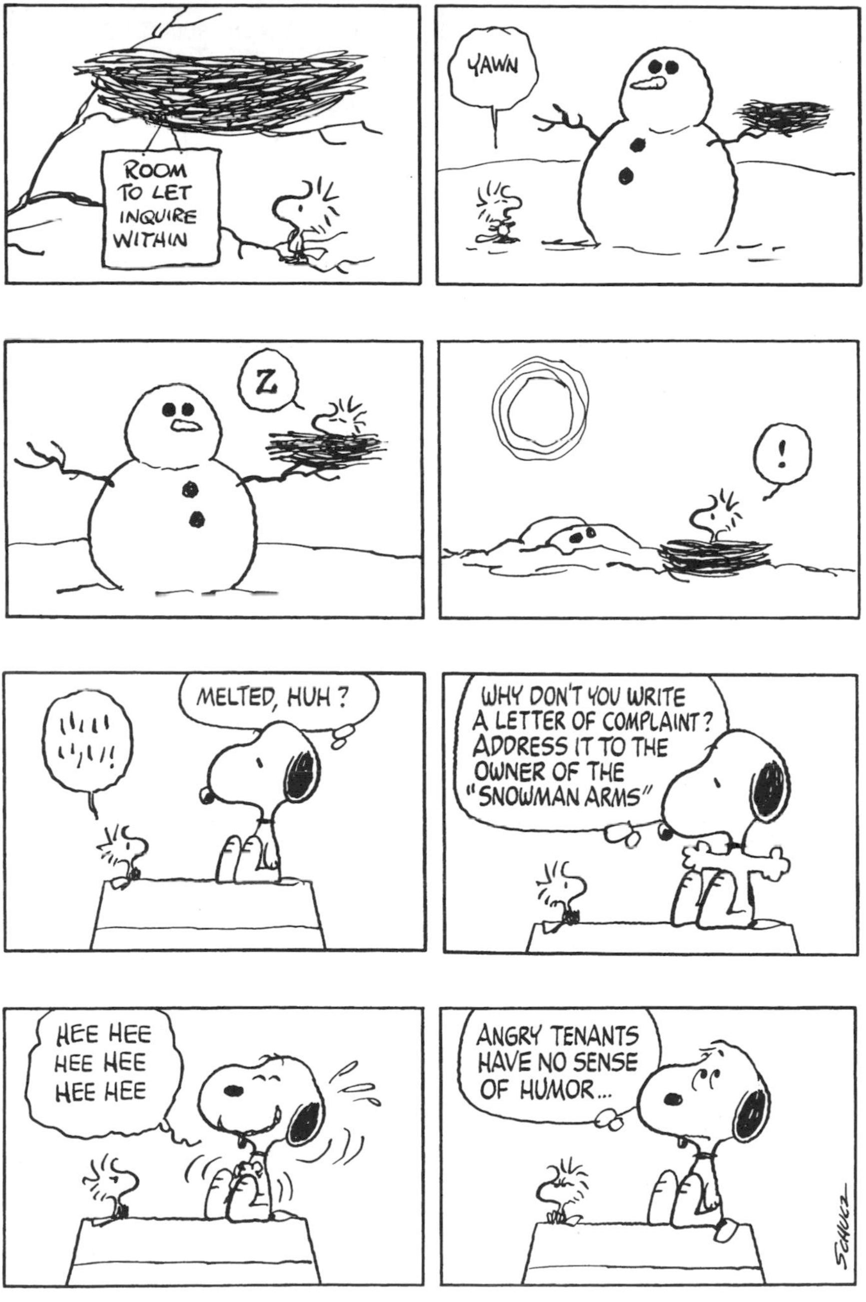
ROOM TO LET INQUIRE WITHIN
YAWN
Z
!
MELTED, HUH ?
WHY DON'T YOU WRITE A LETTER OF COMPLAINT ? ADDRESS IT TO THE OWNER OF THE "SNOWMAN ARMS"
HEE HEE HEE HEE HEE HEE
ANGRY TENANTS HAVE NO SENSE OF HUMOR...
SCHULZ

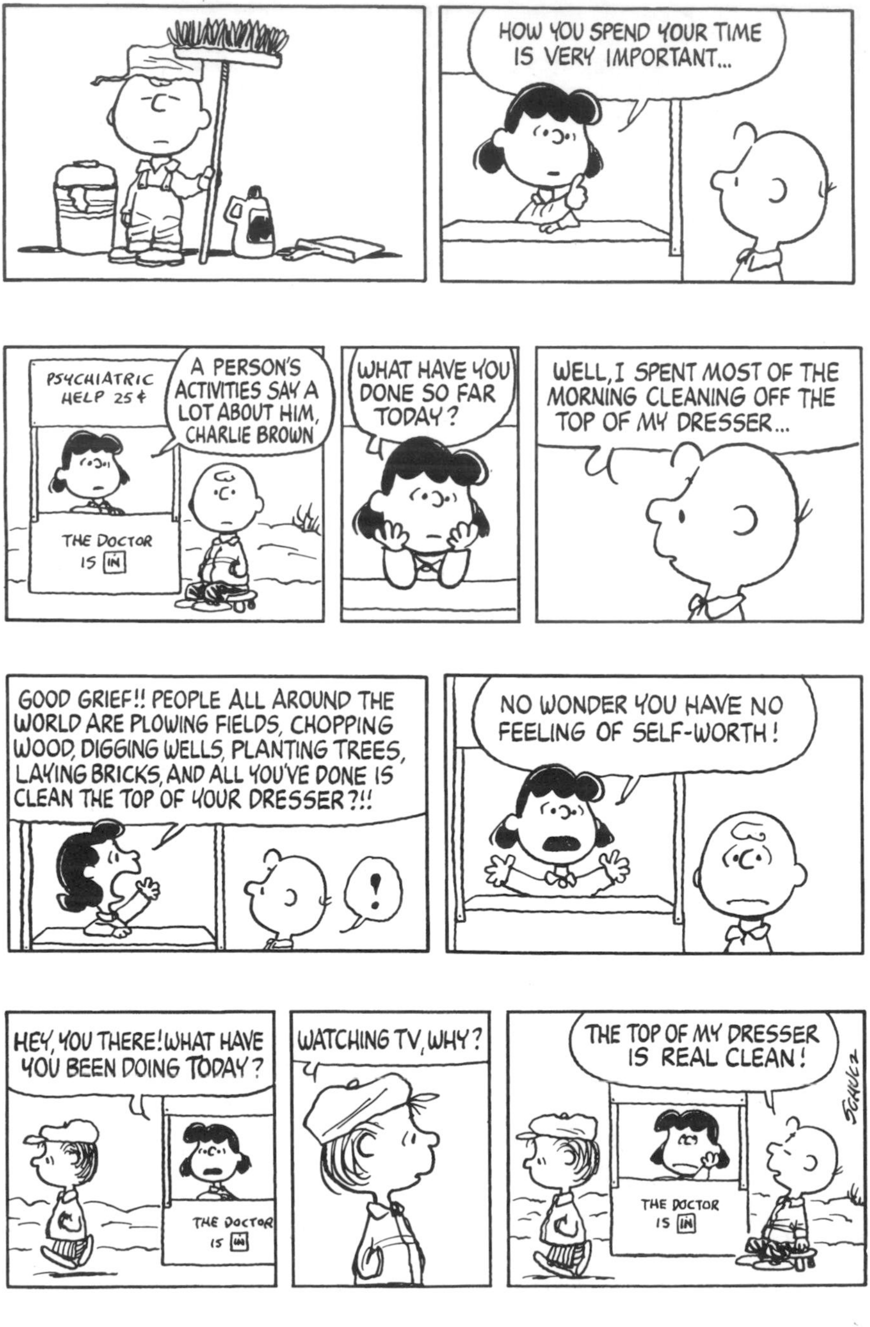
HOW YOU SPEND YOUR TIME IS VERY IMPORTANT...
PSYCHIATRIC HELP 25¢
A PERSON'S ACTIVITIES SAY A LOT ABOUT HIM, CHARLIE BROWN
THE DOCTOR IS IN
WHAT HAVE YOU DONE SO FAR TODAY?
WELL, I SPENT MOST OF THE MORNING CLEANING OFF THE TOP OF MY DRESSER...
GOOD GRIEF!! PEOPLE ALL AROUND THE WORLD ARE PLOWING FIELDS, CHOPPING WOOD, DIGGING WELLS, PLANTING TREES, LAYING BRICKS, AND ALL YOU'VE DONE IS CLEAN THE TOP OF YOUR DRESSER?!!
!
NO WONDER YOU HAVE NO FEELING OF SELF-WORTH!
HEY, YOU THERE! WHAT HAVE YOU BEEN DOING TODAY?
THE DOCTOR IS IN
WATCHING TV, WHY?
THE TOP OF MY DRESSER IS REAL CLEAN!
THE DOCTOR IS IN
SCHULZ

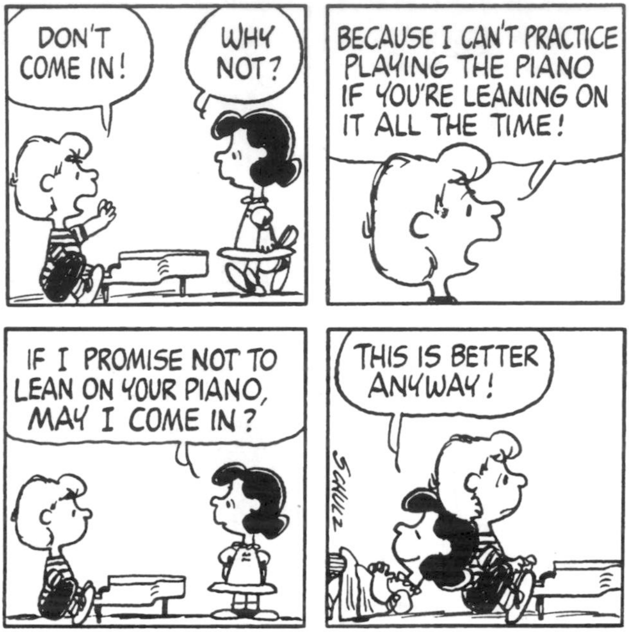
DON'T COME IN!
WHY NOT?
BECAUSE I CAN'T PRACTICE PLAYING THE PIANO IF YOU'RE LEANING ON IT ALL THE TIME!
IF I PROMISE NOT TO LEAN ON YOUR PIANO, MAY I COME IN?
THIS IS BETTER ANYWAY!
SCHULZ

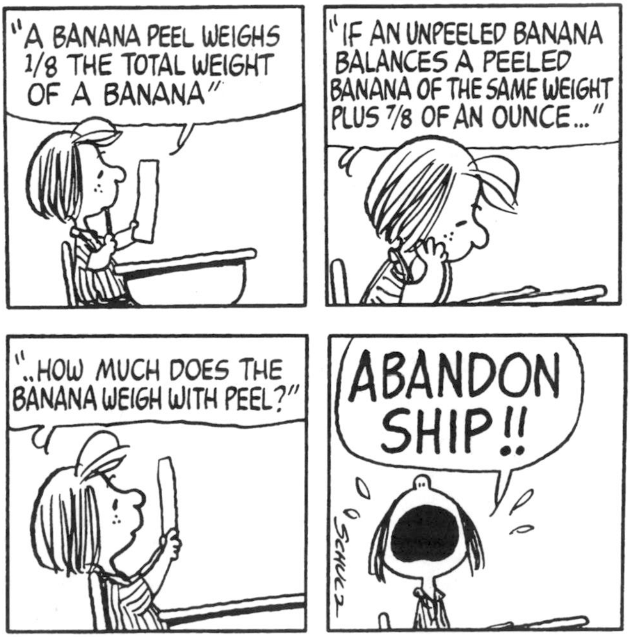
"A BANANA PEEL WEIGHS 1/8 THE TOTAL WEIGHT OF A BANANA"
"IF AN UNPEELED BANANA BALANCES A PEELED BANANA OF THE SAME WEIGHT PLUS 7/8 OF AN OUNCE..."
"..HOW MUCH DOES THE BANANA WEIGH WITH PEEL?"
ABANDON SHIP!!
SCHULZ

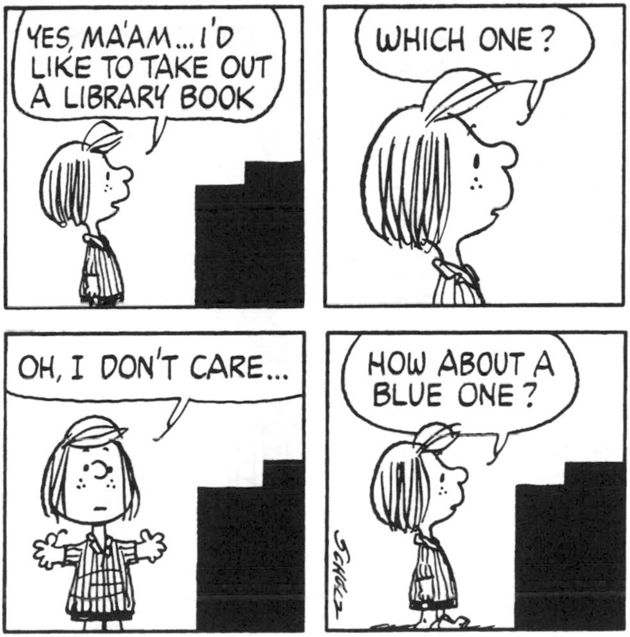
YES, MA'AM... I'D LIKE TO TAKE OUT A LIBRARY BOOK
WHICH ONE?
OH, I DON'T CARE...
HOW ABOUT A BLUE ONE?

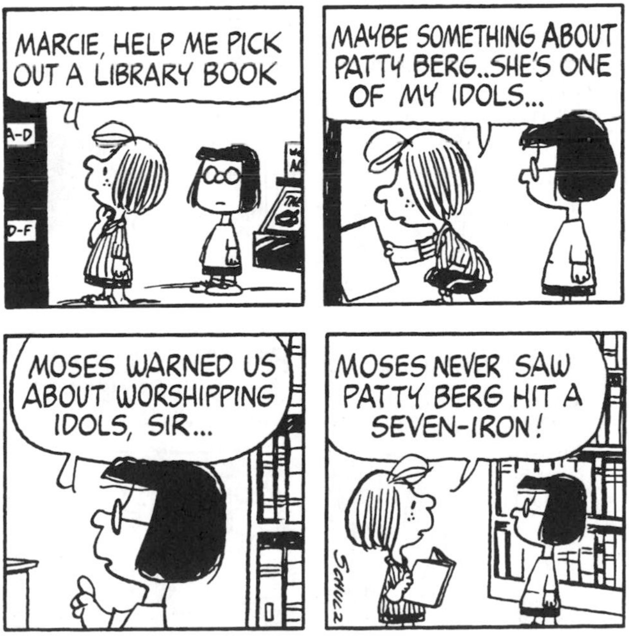
MARCIE, HELP ME PICK OUT A LIBRARY BOOK
A-D
D-F
MAYBE SOMETHING ABOUT PATTY BERG..SHE'S ONE OF MY IDOLS...
MOSES WARNED US ABOUT WORSHIPPING IDOLS, SIR...
MOSES NEVER SAW PATTY BERG HIT A SEVEN-IRON!

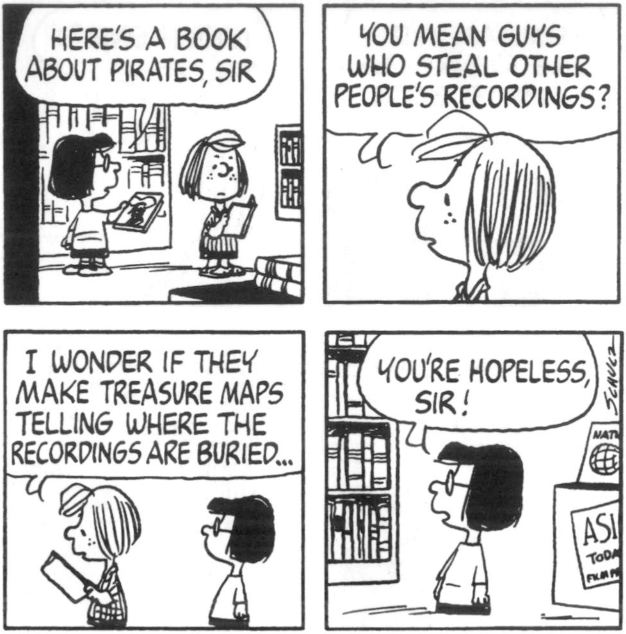
HERE'S A BOOK ABOUT PIRATES, SIR
YOU MEAN GUYS WHO STEAL OTHER PEOPLE'S RECORDINGS?
I WONDER IF THEY MAKE TREASURE MAPS TELLING WHERE THE RECORDINGS ARE BURIED...
YOU'RE HOPELESS, SIR!
SCHULZ

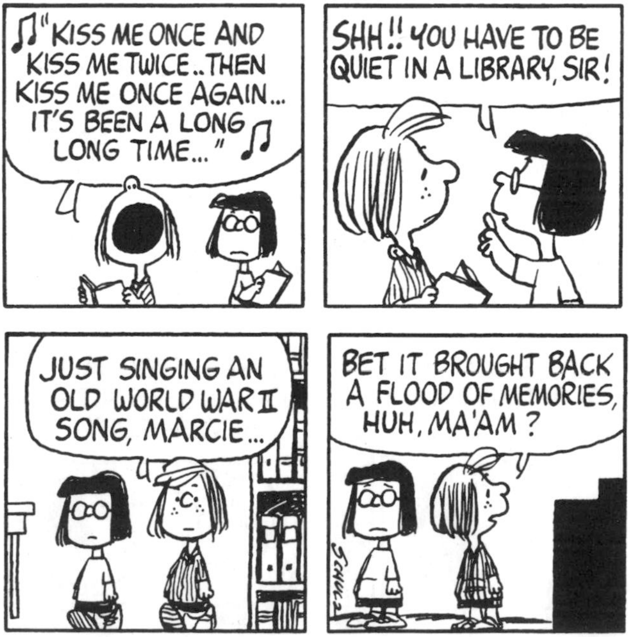
"KISS ME ONCE AND KISS ME TWICE..THEN KISS ME ONCE AGAIN... IT'S BEEN A LONG LONG TIME..."
SHH!! YOU HAVE TO BE QUIET IN A LIBRARY, SIR!
JUST SINGING AN OLD WORLD WAR II SONG, MARCIE...
BET IT BROUGHT BACK A FLOOD OF MEMORIES, HUH, MA'AM?
SCHULZ

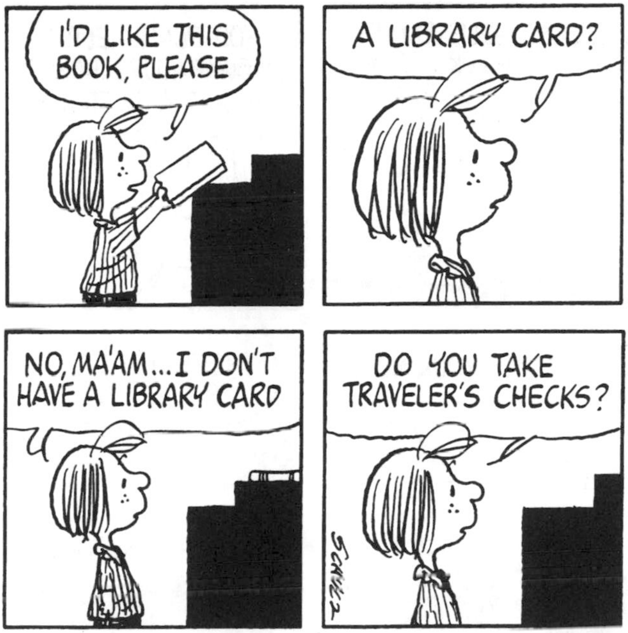
I'D LIKE THIS BOOK, PLEASE
A LIBRARY CARD?
NO, MA'AM... I DON'T HAVE A LIBRARY CARD
DO YOU TAKE TRAVELER'S CHECKS?
SCHULZ

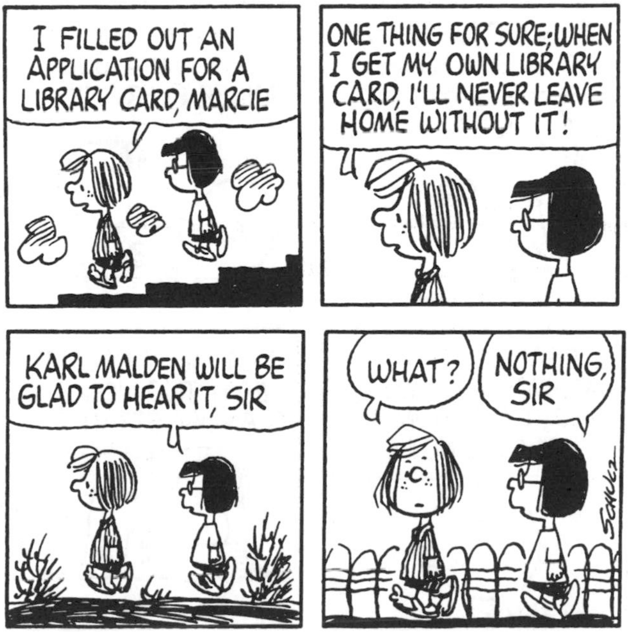
I FILLED OUT AN APPLICATION FOR A LIBRARY CARD, MARCIE
ONE THING FOR SURE; WHEN I GET MY OWN LIBRARY CARD, I'LL NEVER LEAVE HOME WITHOUT IT!
KARL MALDEN WILL BE GLAD TO HEAR IT, SIR
WHAT?
NOTHING, SIR
SCHULZ